MARITIME COOPERATION BETWEEN INDIA AND SRI LANKA

The Regional Centre for Strategic Studies (RCSS) is an independent, non-profit and non-governmental organization for collaborative research, networking and interaction on strategic and international issues pertaining to South Asia. Set up in 1992, the RCSS is based in Colombo, Sri Lanka.

The RCSS is a South Asian forum for studies, training and multi-track dialogue and deliberation on issues of regional interest. All activities of RCSS are designed with a South Asia focus and are usually participated by experts from all South Asian countries. The Centre is envisaged as a forum for advancing the cause of cooperation, security, conflict resolution, confidence building, peace and development in the countries of the South Asian region.

The RCSS serves its South Asian and international constituency by: (a) networking programmes that promote interaction, communication and exchange between institutions and individuals within and outside the region engaged in South Asian strategic studies; (b) organizing regional workshops and seminars and sponsoring and coordinating collaborative research; and (c) disseminating output of the research through publications which include books, monographs and a quarterly newsletter. The RCSS facilitates scholars and other professionals of South Asia to address, mutually and collectively, problems and issues of topical interest for all countries of the region.

Queries may be addressed to:

Regional Centre for Strategic Studies
2 Elibank Road
Colombo 5
SRI LANKA
Tel: (94-11) 2599734, 2599735
Fax: 2599993; e-mail: rcss@sri.lanka.net
RCSS website: http://www.rcss.org

RCSS Policy Studies 36

Maritime Cooperation between India and Sri Lanka

ADLURI SUBRAMANYAM RAJU
S.I. KEETHAPONCALAN

REGIONAL CENTRE FOR STRATEGIC STUDIES
COLOMBO

MANOHAR
2006

Published by
Ajay Kumar Jain *for*
Manohar Publishers & Distributors
4753/23 Ansari Road, Daryaganj
New Delhi 110 002
and
Regional Centre for Strategic Studies
2 Elibank Road
Colombo 5
SRI LANKA
Tel: (94-11) 2599734-5; Fax: 2599993;
e-mail: rcss@sri.lanka.net
Website: http://www.rcss.org

First published 2006

ISBN 81-7304-690-5

Typeset by
Kohli Print
Delhi 110 051

Printed at
Lordson Publishers Pvt. Ltd.
Delhi 110 007

Distributed in South Asia by
FOUNDATION BOOKS
4381/4, Ansari Rorad
Daryaganj, New Delhi 110 002
and its branches at Mumbai, Hyderabad,
Bangalore, Chennai, Kolkata

Contents

Acknowledgements

It is our foremost duty to express our sincere gratitude to the Regional Center for Strategic Studies (RCSS) for supporting this research project. We express our deep sense of indebtedness to Professor Sridhar Khatri, Executive Director of RCSS, for his encouragement and help in completing the project. But for his wholehearted support this project would not have completed. The Mahbub-ul-Haq Award was made possible becuse of the generous funding from the Ford Foundation. Our sincere appreciation also goes to the Ford Foundation.

We would be failing in our duty if we do not acknowledge the contribution and support of many people, experts, fishermen, who helped us during our field study.

We would like to express our gratitude to Professor Isaac Sequeira, Professor P.V. Rao, Dr. J.L.N. Rao, S. Srinivas Rao, Profesor V. Suryanarayan, H.E. Sumith Nakandala, Dr. V. Vivekanandan, Antony Benchilas, Commodore R.S. Vasan, Arulanandam and G. Ramesh for thier sustained support.

ADLURI SUBRAMANYAM RAJU
S.I. KEETHAPONCALAN

RCSS is grateful to the
Ford Foundation for its generous
support for the Mahbub-ul-Haq Award
on which this report is based.

CHAPTER 1

Introduction

India and Sri Lanka, the former colonies of the British, obtained Independence in 1947 and 1948 respectively. India, in terms of geographical size, economy and geopolitical location, occupies a pivotal position in the Indian Ocean region. It has maritime borders with Pakistan, the Maldives, Sri Lanka, and Bangladesh. Sri Lanka an island country, shares maritime borders with India and the Maldives.

The two countries share common interests in keeping the region free from conflict and external interference. There have been times though, when Sri Lanka has supported the presence of external powers in the Indian Ocean region because it perceived a threat from India, and also to deal with the internal security problems created by armed groups in its south and north. Though India and Sri Lanka have agreements to demarcate their boundaries, they have differences over some maritime issues. The maritime boundary of India and Sri Lanka is divided at three different points in different seas: the Bay of Bengal in the north, the Palk Straits in the middle, and the Gulf of Mannar in the south. The maximum distance between these two countries though the Palk Straits is about 45 km. and the minimum distance is around 16 km. between Dhanushkodi on the Indian side and Thalaimannar on the Sri Lankan coast. They don't have Exclusive Economic Zones (EEZ) in the area. They have rights over 12 to 22 km. of water. Crossing that area means crossing the international boundary line rather than the EEZ. The coasts of both countries is larger in the Bay of Bengal and in the Gulf of Mannar. The Palk Straits is shallow waters and its depth is not beyond 50 m at any point. In the south the bay is narrower and Adam's Bridge which connects Dhanushkodi and Thalaimannar acts as a barrier to the Gulf of Mannar (see Map 1). The countries signed bilateral agreements on the Maritime boundary in June 1974 and on the maritime boundary in the Gulf of Mannar and the Bay of Bengal in March 1976. They also signed a Supplementary Agreement in November 1976 on the extension of the maritime boundary between the two countries in the Gulf of Mannar from position 13m to the trijunction point between India, Sri Lanka and the Maldives (Point T).

THE PROBLEM

Differences between India and Sri Lanka on maritime issues began after the United Nations Conference on the Law of the Sea-III (UNCLOS-III) agreement in 1982. The distance between India and Sri Lanka, from a place like Rameswaram (India) is only 15 to 20 km. India recognized Sri Lanka's sovereignty over Kachchativu Island, and, in return, Sri Lanka recognized India's sovereignty over Wadge Bank in 1976. Later in 1980s Sri Lanka began objecting to Indian fishermen moving in the region adjacent to Kachchativu Island, which adversely affected the livelihood of many Indian fishermen. The mining and fishing rights of both countries around Kachchativu Island became contentious issues.

Ever since civil war broke out in Sri Lanka, the maritime zone between India and Sri Lanka has become turbulent, affecting the interests of both countries. Apart from the disturbances caused by the illegal movement of Tamil groups, frequent incidents of attacks on fishermen, smuggling of illicit weapons, drugs, piratical activities and assaults on security forces by the Tamil guerrillas have been the norm. The northern coast of Sri Lanka, Velveltiturai and Mannar district has served as centres for the smugglers. On the Indian side, Tuticorin, Pattukotiai, Rameswaram, Tiruchendur, and Nagapatnam have figured as bases for smuggling. It is reported that illegal trade goes on from Sri Lanka to India and the Gulf of Mannar and vice versa through their waters. In this context, there is a greater need to enhance mutual cooperation in maritime security. Such cooperation may include measures such as joint naval patrolling, controlling of smuggling and piratical activities, and the strengthening of communication networks. Through cooperation, both countries can exploit living and non-living resources, shipbuilding, weather forecasting, prevention of pollution, and combat maritime terrorism, which are the responsibilities of every country. Apart from such measures, there is a greater potential for enhancing and institutionalizing economic cooperation in the exploration and exploitation of sea resources in the Indian Ocean waters. A few steps have already been initiated by both countries to extend cooperation in some of the above areas. Yet, a more organized thrust is needed to enhance and institutionalize maritime cooperation between the two countries.

This study has analysed the various maritime issues between India and Sri Lanka.

OBJECTIVES

This study focuses on the following objectives:

1. Examining the prospects for the settlement of the maritime dispute between India and Sri Lanka.
2. Analysing the potential areas of maritime cooperation in the EEZ, deep-sea resource exploration, and bilateral understanding on respective fishermen's problems.
3. Examining security threats from illegal networks.
4. Analysing the Indo-Sri Lankan joint initiatives towards regional maritime security management in the Bay of Bengal.

SIGNIFICANCE OF THE STUDY

The study is important for the promotion of better understanding between India and Sri Lanka on maritime issues. The project focuses on the reasonable options available to both countries. It may bring out a new perspective on the problem between a larger and a smaller country. Moreover, some of the issues in maritime relations directly and indirectly affect lives of communities in and around the coastal areas. A systematic analysis of these issues may improve understanding of the dynamics of the problems at hand among policy-makers, most of whom are largely disconnected from the ground realities. Such an understanding may help resolve some of the problems faced by these communities.

METHODOLOGY

The study is descriptive and analytical, based on primary and secondary sources. Primary sources are agreements and interviews. Secondary sources include books, articles, and newspapers. We [Adluri Subramanyam Raju from India, and S.I. Keethaponcalan from Sri Lanka] carried out surveys in our respective countries—India and Sri Lanka. Field investigations in the adjacent coastal areas were carried out of ten villages in Mannar district (Sri Lanka), and Tuticorin, Rameswaram, Tiruchendur, Nagapatnam, Chennai [earlier Madras], and Thiruvananthapuram [earlier Trivandrum; India]. We stayed in the coastal areas for a short period to observe the attitudes of some of the people who were involved in the maritime issues between the two countries. Hence, the field research component was constituted primarily of observation and interview methods. An interview schedule was used to elicit views from fishermen, coast guards, NGOs and scholars on maritime issues of both countries. The study tried to find out the differences of opinion on the problem.

CHAPTER 2

Maritime Issues between India and Sri Lanka

At the time of Independence or in the immediate post-Independence era, India and Sri Lanka did not have maritime boundaries officially demarcated as both were ruled by one imperial power. After Independence, it was found necessary to define their maritime jurisdictions. Unfortunately, neither India nor Sri Lanka felt the need to consult the other in their attempt to determine their respective maritime zones. India unilaterally extended its territorial waters from 3 to 6 nautical miles (nm) in 1956, and later, in 1957, claimed jurisdiction over a contiguous area of 100 nm from its territorial waters. Sri Lanka also unilaterally extended its own jurisdiction to 6 nm and a contiguous area of 100 nm. A further extension was made by both the countries in 1967 to include 12 miles of waters under their maritime jurisdiction, obviously exacerbating the tension in bilateral relations.

Later, both countries signed agreements on maritime boundaries in the 1970s (see Introduction). These agreements to an extent diluted the intensity of differences between the two States and contributed to improving relations.

In this chapter, an attempt has been made to examine issues such as the security concerns of India and Sri Lanka; the Indian Ocean as a Zone of Peace; the Kachchativu issue; fishermen's problems; the land bridge and Sethusamudram Ship Canal Project; the threat from the Sea Tigers; Tamil refugee problem; economic cooperation; and energy cooperation between India and Sri Lanka.

SECURITY CONCERNS OF INDIA AND SRI LANKA

K.M. Panikkar, former Indian diplomat, has argued that since the sixteenth century, India has faced a threat from the sea and it would continue to do so in the future. He stresses the importance of protecting the maritime assets. Regarding India's need to develop its naval force in the region, he stated that:

> India's security lies on the Indian Ocean, that without a well considered and effective naval policy, India's position in the world will be weak, dependent on others and her freedom at the mercy of any country capable of controlling the Indian Ocean. India's future, therefore, is closely bound up with the strength she is able to develop gradually as a naval power.[1]

By virtue of its position in the Indian Ocean, India has to play an active role promoting maritime security of the region, for instance, in partnership with other powers in the region.

External military presence in the Indian Ocean is a matter of deep concern to India.[2] As a regional power, India has initiated certain steps to promote peace in the region. It also has to protect the interests of people of Indian origin living in different parts of the region, viz., in Mauritius, the Reunion Islands, and Seychelles.[3] The external military presence in the region poses not only a threat to the region, but also a major constraint on its role in the area. It is also a threat to India's economic interests as it imports two-thirds of its crude oil from the West Asian Gulf region. Its merchant marine possesses 890 vessels of a total of 6,516,780 tonnes traversing the Indian Ocean region and is thus dependent on the sea for its trade.[4] India has 27 major warships and 12 major ports to defend its 7,500 km. coastline. The Indian Navy has 12 fast patrol boats and only some of them are deployed in sensitive areas like the Palk Straits, where there is a possibility of threat from the Sea Tigers.[5]

[1] Cited in K.M. Panikkar, *India and the Indian Ocean*, Bombay [now Mumbai]: George Allen Unwin, 1945, p. 92.

[2] For further details, see A. Subramanyam Raju, *Democracies at Loggerheads: Security Aspects of US–India Relations*, Colorado: International Academic Publishers, and New Delhi: South Asian Publishers, 2001, pp. 75–100.

[3] For details, see A. Subramanyam Raju, 'French Economic and Strategic Interests in the Western Indian Ocean Region: 1975–1990', *Journal of Indian Ocean Studies*, vol. 5, no. 1, November 1997, pp. 21–34.

[4] Ibid., p. 79.

[5] K.R. Singh, 'Defining Non-State Actors': www.asthabharati.org/Dia_Apr03/krs.htm

India imports about two-thirds of its oil from the Gulf region and also imports natural gas and sulphur from West Asia and exports tea, tobacco, spices, vegetables, fruits, meat, jute, iron ore, engineering goods, leather, medicines, and defence equipment to West Asia. Under UNCLOS-III, nearly 20,00,000 sq. km. of area has come under India's jurisdiction. India has been recognized as a pioneer investor in ocean mining. India was given the status of a pioneer nation in 1987 to explore and exploit the resources of the seabed. India has been allocated 150,000 sq. km. of seabed by the UN Seabed Authority for mining in the central Indian Ocean which is only 384 km. away from the island of Diego Garcia an important American military base in the Indian Occan.[6] Thus, it has became necessary for India to strengthen its navy to defend its economic and strategic interests.[7]

Nevertheless, most of the littoral states has perceived India's efforts to build a strong navy as its desire to play a 'big brother' role in the region.[8] Although Indian leaders have on many occasions explicitly stated that India is not aspiring for such a role, some littoral states have continued to harbour doubts about India's naval expansion plans and objectives. For instance, Sri Lanka believes that India, being a regional power, would like to dominate the region.[9] This sentiment was extremely strong in the 1980s.

[6] Kenneth R. Simmondes, *New Directions in the Law of the Sea*, London: Oceana Publications, 1988, pp. 9, 16.

[7] It has 2.015 million sq. km. of EEZ of which 30 per cent lies in the region of the Andaman & Nicobar Islands. It was estimated that the stock of fish was between 50,000 and 100,000 tonnes in the area of 129,000 nautical sq. miles. It was estimated that 453,000 sq. km. of EEZ contain about 40 million tonnes of fish and about one billion tonnes of oil. The West Coast region was estimated to have 570 oil-bearing structures, of which 176 have been confirmed and 81 discovered. See S.L. Rao, 'Geopolitical and Economic Realities of the West Coast of India' , in *Indian Ocean: Challenges and Opportunities*, ed. S.L. Rao, New Delhi: Navy Foundation, 1992, p. 50.

[8] Its two military conflicts with Pakistan, the capture of Goa from Portugal, the peaceful nuclear explosion in 1974, its involvement in the Sri Lankan ethnic problem (in the 1980s), were instances of the manifestation of power that made others suspect India's power game/adherence to peaceful norms.

[9] *Bangkok Post*, 14 December 1974, cited in A. Subramanyam Raju, 'United States (US) and South Asia: A Study with Reference to US Policy Towards India 1969-1988', Ph.D. thesis, University of Hyderabad, 1998, pp. 124–5.

A great threat to the national integrity of the State of Sri Lanka emerged when radical Tamil youth got involved in a movement to set up a separate State in the northern and the eastern provinces. The Tamils sought help from Tamil Nadu in India, both moral and financial. There are about 60 million Tamils living in this State. In fact, India was a role model for the Sri Lankan Tamils even before Tamil politics turned violent. S.J.V. Chelvanayaga's movement for greater autonomy for the Tamil region was modelled on Gandhi's *satyagraha* campaign, and moderate Tamil leaders traditionally maintained close relationships with political leaders in Tamil Nadu. Therefore, even at an early stage, the Sinhalese in Sri Lanka perceived India and the Tamils as one and the same. Some Sinhalese even believed that all Indians are Tamils. The linkage between Sri Lankan Tamils and India further strengthened when Tamil militants began to get assistance from Tamil Nadu for their violent campaign in Sri Lanka. The 32 km. wide Palk Straits could be easily crossed in a short time by boat. The people of Tamil Nadu, who were highly sympathetic to the Tamil cause in Sri Lanka, began to fund and extend their assistance in more concrete ways, at times with the assistance of public servants, including the police. These activities culminated in the setting up of training camps for the Tamil militants in Tamil Nadu and elsewhere with the explicit concurrence of the Government of Tamil Nadu and later the Indian central government. Sri Lanka opposed India's involvement as the Tamil issue in Sri Lanka was considered an internal issue.

Sentiments against India among the Sinhala population were widespread then. The Sri Lankan Navy shared the view that India was a threat to the sovereignty and territorial integrity of Sri Lanka. Following the Sri Lankan Armed Forces attempt to gain control of the territories held by the Liberation Tigers of Tamil Eelam (LTTE, or 'Tigers') in the north, code-named Operation Liberation, India directly came to the defence of the Tigers in the guise of humanitarian assistance. India sent shiploads of relief supplies to the war-ravaged north by sea, which was a violation of the sovereignty of Sri Lanka. The Indian Air

Force dropped food by air in an operation code-named Operation Poomalai as an expression of sympathy for the Tamils in Sri Lanka.

Later, India and Sri Lanka signed an accord in 1987. This paved the way for the deployment of the Indian Peace Keeping Force (IPKF) to ensure implementation of the agreement. In spite of the policy shift in India in favour of the Sri Lankan State, the image of India as a 'Tamil friend' did not change to a great extent among the Sinhalese. When Ranasinghe Premadasa became the President of Sri Lanka, the IPKF was asked to withdraw from Sri Lanka.

This extremely uneasy relationship began to change with a series of incidents in the early 1990s and culminated when Chandrika Kumaratunga became the President of Sri Lanka. However, the assassination of Rajiv Gandhi by an LTTE suicide bomber brought with it shock and a change in policy. In addition, the introduction of the Gujral Doctrine in India led to cordial relations between the two countries. As far as the ethnic conflict is concerned, although India has adopted a policy of non-interference, collaboration on the military front has improved tremendously. President Kumaratunga now holds clout and the respect of foreign policy circles in Delhi. The Indian image as a friend has improved immensely in Colombo. Accordingly, the Sri Lankan Navy's perceptions about India has also changed, which has had an impact on the way the Navy handles Indian fisherman in the mid-seas.

THE INDIAN OCEAN AS A ZONE OF PEACE (IOZP)

In early 1970, one of the issues that showed and had potential for greater cooperation between Sri Lanka and India was the former's proposal for declaring the Indian Ocean as a zone of peace. But as changes occurred in the political apparatus and of perceptions in Sri Lanka, this got diluted, leading to loss of an opportunity for bilateral cooperation. Sirimavo Bandaranaike urged UN Secretary General Kurt Waldheim in 1971 to include the IOZP proposal in the agenda of the 26th Session of the General Assembly.[10] While speaking in the General Assembly on the issue, she maintained that her proposal was intended as a direct and tangible contribution to disarmament and to the strengthening of conditions for world peace.[11] On 16 December 1971, the UN General Assembly passed a resolution declaring the IOZP.[12] The first operative paragraph dealt with the implementation of the IOZP.[13] The second operative paragraph called on the great powers to consult the littoral States of the Indian Ocean to halt further escalation and expansion of their military presence in the Indian Ocean and to eliminate all bases, military installations and logistical supply facilities, the disposition of nuclear weapons and weapons of mass destruction, and any manifestation of great-power military presence in the region.[14] The third paragraph called upon the littoral and hinterland States of the Indian Ocean, the permanent members of the UN Security Council and other major maritime users of the region to ensure that warships and military aircraft should not use the Indian Ocean for any threat or use of force against the sovereignty, territorial integrity, and independence of any littoral and hinterland State of the Indian Ocean, and arrangements were to be made for the maintenance of the IOZP. In 1972, the Assembly also decided to establish an ad hoc committee consisting of 15 members to study the implications of the proposal with special reference to the practical measures that might be

[10] For details, see *United Nations General Assembly Official Records*, 26th Session, 1971 (Annexes), Document A/8584. Report of the first committee on Agenda Item 98, 14 December 1971, New York: United Nations.

[11] Ibid.

[12] Resolution 2832 (XXVI) was adopted by a vote of 61-0 with 55 abstentions, regarding the first operative paragraph of the resolution. See *UNGAOR*, 2022nd plenary meeting, 16 December 1976, Agenda Item 98. The second and third operative paragraphs were supported by a vote of 43-0 with 55 abstentions. On the same day, voting was held once again and this time the first operative paragraph was passed by a vote of 60-0 with 55 abstentions. The second and third operative paragraphs were approved by a vote of 52-0 with 63 abstaining.

[13] *UN Year Book 1971*, vol. 25, New York: United Nations, p. 35.

[14] Ibid.

taken to further the objectives of the 1971 Declaration.[15] The Declaration gave due regard to the security interests of the littoral and hinterland States of the Indian Ocean and the interests of any other State consistent with the purposes and principles of the UN Charter.[16]

The vast size of the Indian Ocean, tri-continental dimension, and diversity among the littoral states in ethnicity and culture ensured that they did not adopt and follow a single strategic stance. Most of the countries in the region have conflicts with their neighbours, viz., India, Pakistan, Afghanistan, Iran, Iraq, Kuwait, Thailand, Malaysia, Indonesia, Jordan, Egypt, Somalia and Ethiopia. Candid differences of opinion have existed amongst them regarding the presence of the great powers in this region. Most of the littoral States opined that in the absence of a great-power military presence, India, Indonesia and Iran, being larger countries in the region, would dominate the region. They preferred the presence of the great powers to check the dominance of the regional powers.

Though the idea of the IOZP first came from Sri Lanka, it later did not show much interest in implementing the proposal in the Indian Ocean because of its apprehensions about India.

Sri Lanka maintained that in the interdependent world of the day, the great powers couldn't accept the whole of Asia to be under the control of one country. It emphasized that it was better to depend on some kind of a strategic balance being established by the great powers to ensure that there was no hegemony of any single power in the Indian Ocean region. Sri Lanka, with Singapore and Australia, called for a 'balanced presence' of external powers in the region.[17] Thus, the country which initiated the

[15] Resolution 2992 (XXVII) was passed by a vote of 95-0 with 33 abstentions on 15 December 1972. See *UN Year Book 1972*, New York: United Nations, 1972, p. 28. The ad hoc committee members were: Australia, China, India, Indonesia, Iran, Iraq, Japan, Madagascar, Malaysia, Mauritius, Pakistan, Sri Lanka, Tanzania, Yemen, and Zambia.

[16] Ibid.

[17] Adi H. Doctor, 'India's Indian Ocean Policy', *Indian Journal of Political Science* (Madras [now Chennai]), vol. 51, no. 3, July–September 1990, p. 375.

concept of the IOZP changed its stand because of its fears of a big neighbour and the proposal became a dead letter.

KACHCHATIVU ISLAND

Kachchativu is one of the thorny issues that continue to disturb good-neighbourly relations between the two countries. Kachchativu Island is 1 mile long, 300 yards broad, and has an area of 285.2 acres. The British had used this island since 1920 as a naval gunnery practice range. It is a barren, uninhabited place and without drinking water. The island has a Catholic church dedicated to St. Anthony, considered the guardian of fishermen. It was belived that the church was constructed by Seenikuppam Padayachi, a fisherman from Ramanathapuram into early twentieth century. The fishermen and pilgrims of both countries used to visit the church in March every year for a religious festival, in the belief that St. Anthony would protect them from turbulent seas and inclement weather. People from northern Sri Lanka and Tamil Nadu used to share their culture and ideas. Historically, the fishermen communities of both countries have similarities. They speak Tamil and have continued to maintain relations for centuries. There was free movement of people before Independence and it continued till 1974. After the 1974 and 1976 agreements and the eruption of civil war in Sri Lanka in 1983, the situation changed entirely and the relationship between the peoples of the two countries underwent a transformation.

Though the island is barren and uninhabited, its surroundings have an abundance of prawns. The island is not strategically important for India. But, for Indian fishermen it is a very important place associated with their livelihood. After Independence, Sri Lanka claimed rights over the island. In 1965, it planned to use the island for aerial practice and firing. It requested India not to allow its planes to fly over the area.

Madras state claimed ownership of the island on the basis of the rights enjoyed by the zamindar of Ramnad. The zamindar not only owned the island, but also leased it from time to time to various parties for the exploration of marine resources. Sri Lanka, on the other hand, claims ownership on various factors. For instance, Sri Lanka maintains that:

1. The St. Anthony's church on the island traditionally belongs to the Jaffna Diocese;
2. Old Dutch colonial maps and records (1665) shows the island as part of Jaffna Pattanam;
3. In 1876, the survey officers of the Government of India treated Kachchativu as part of Ceylon;
4. A 1915 report relating to triangulation in India and adjacent countries treated the island as part of Jaffna taluk;
5. In a letter dated 8 March 1923, the Government of India confirmed Ceylon's claim over the island; and
6. During Second World War, the Royal Navy requested permission from the Government of Ceylon (not India) to conduct military training.[18]

The Indian government, however, did have some doubts regarding the Ramnad zamindar's rights over the island and apparently did not have much interest in maintaining it under its control. In his speech in the Rajya Sabha in September 1960, Jawaharlal Nehru, Prime Minister of India, said: 'There was a claim on one of the old principal Zamindaris and it was part of the Zamindari. The Zamindari has gone now and I do not know where the matter stands.'[19] He replied to a question in the Rajya Sabha: 'The Island is 18 miles east of Pamban. Where Pamban is I do not know.'[20] Later, Prime Minister Indira Gandhi said that since both countries had cordial relations, it was not wise to raise a voice over the island.[21] She felt that the island was a 'sheer rock with no strategic significance'. She did not even bother to consult

[18] P.K. Balachandran, 'Fishing in Troubled Waters', *Hindustan Times*, 15 March 2003.

[19] *Rajya Sabha Debates*, New Delhi: Parliament Secretariat, 1 September 1960, cols. 3049–50.

[20] Ibid., col. 3050.

[21] *Hindustan Times*, 2 March 1968, cited in V. Suryanarayan, *Kachchativu and the Problems of Indian Fishermen in the Palk Bay Region*, Chennai: T. R. Publications, 1994, p. 17.

the Tamil Nadu government regarding the island. In 1974, India and Sri Lanka signed an agreement which ensured the sovereign right of Sri Lanka over the disputed island of Kachchativu.

THE 1974 AGREEMENT

The 1974 agreement has two clauses, which protect a few activities of the Indian fishermen. Article 5 maintains that, 'Subject to the foregoing, the Indian fishermen and pilgrims will enjoy access to visit Kachchativu as *hitherto* and will not be required by Sri Lanka to obtain travel documents or Visas for these purposes.' Article 6 of the agreement states that, 'The vessels of Sri Lanka and India will enjoy each other's Waters such rights as they have enjoyed therein.'

The two articles talked only about access to the island by the fishermen and rights of sea-going vessels of both countries. Neither Article 5 nor 6 specifically talked about the Indian fishermen's rights near the island. However, during the discussion in the Lok Sabha, Swaran Singh, the then Minister for External Affairs, maintained that the fishing rights of Indian fishermen were protected and he cited the 1921 agreement, according to which 'the Western side of the fishery line was the exclusive fishery right of the Indian citizens and to the east of that was the right of Sri Lanka fishermen. But in spite of that division, the fishermen generally were free to fish even round about Kachchativu and they also used the Kachchativu Island for drying their nets. . . .' On the question of fishermen's rights, Singh continued, 'although Sri Lanka's claim to sovereignty over Kachchativu has been recognized, the traditional rights of Indian fishermen and pilgrims to visit the island remain unaffected'.[22] From this statement, one can understand that India believed that the Indian fishermen had rights to fish around the island.

According to the 1974 agreement, the Indian fishermen and pilgrims would continue to enjoy their traditional rights. How-

[22] *Lok Sabha Debates*, New Delhi: Parliament Secretariat, 23 July 1974, cols. 200–201.

ever, the Sri Lankan government did not subscribe to the Indian government's view. It argued that the agreement did not give any fishing rights, but only the rights to dry their fishing nets, to rest, and to the right of pilgrims to visit the island for religious purposes. The agreement was drafted in such a way that it can lead to ambiguity.

Sri Lanka maintains that the island has belonged to it over the centuries. Way back in the times of the Raj, on 24 October 1921, officials of Madras Presidency and Ceylon met to discuss the demarcation of the Palk Straits and the Gulf of Mannar. The Ceylonese official, Horsburgh, proposed that delimitation should 'follow the median line, subject to an incursion beyond that line so as to include the islet of Kachchativu and three miles to the westward'.[23] But due to no clear instructions from the British Indian government, the delegation could not proceed further. They mentioned that the island was within the zamindari of Ramnad. Sri Lanka claimed that the Indian government acknowledged Ceylon's claim over the island. But India did not accept Sri Lanka's claim. In later years, Dinesh Singh, the then Minister of State for External Affairs, during the discussion on the issue in the Rajya Sabha in May 1956 said that, 'There was a meeting in 1921, in which there was the representative from the government of Madras and they had agreed that while the Zamindari rights of the Raja of Ramnad would continue, the island belonged to Ceylon. The fact was not accepted by the Secretary of State for India and since then the dispute has been going on.'[24] Arulanandam, Secretary of the Rameswaram Verkottu Fishermen's Association, in an interview with one of the authors said that 'India had made a blunder regarding handing over the Kachchativu Island to Sri Lanka.' He questioned the Indian government giving away the island to Sri Lanka without consulting the Tamil Nadu government and the people of Tamil Nadu.[25] However, the fishermen in Rameswaram

[23] Cited in Suryanarayan, n. 21, op. cit., p. 11.

[24] *Rajya Sabha Debates*, New Delhi: Parliament Secretariat, 17 May 1966, cols. 1683–4.

[25] Arulanandan, in an interview to one of the authors, Pamban, 29 November 2003.

and Pamban told one of the authors in an interview that they were not bothered about who controlled the island, but were insistent upon the restoration of their old rights to fish around the island.[26] For them, the boundary did not matter, but livelihood was important. The views expressed by B.P. Peiris, the then Secretary to the Cabinet of Ceylon need to be noted here. He argued:

I remember coming across the problem when I was an Assistant Legal Draftsman. I had to deal with a file for the purpose of verifying some of the boundaries of the northern district. In the process of revising the draft proclamation, I had to trace the history of the boundary back over many years. I remember coming across a proclamation issued, probably in the time of Queen Victoria, in which the island of Kachchativu is excluded from the northern district as it belonged to the Raja of Ramnad.[27]

Further, a researcher from Sri Lanka in her thesis mentioned that the demarcation of the island was based on the agreement rather than on the equidistance principle. However, Shelton Kodikara, Sri Lankan expert on international relations, summarizes the agreement as follows:

The agreement demarcated a boundary in the sea from a point about 18 nm north-west of Point Pedra in Palk Strait to Adams Bridge, a distance of approximately 86 nm. The agreement gave each country sovereignty and exclusive jurisdiction over the land and waters on its side of the boundary line. The vessels of each country were to enjoy in each other's water the right of navigation as they had traditionally enjoyed, while each country was to be free to explore and exploit all petroleum and mineral resources falling on its side of the boundary. Provision was made for the two countries to agree on the method of most effective exploration where the petroleum or mineral deposits were found to extend from one side of the boundary to the other.[28]

[26] Interviews with the fishermen of Rameswaram by one of the authors, 29–30 November 2003; and Pamban, 1–2 December 2003.

[27] *Statesman*, 12 May 1966, cited in Suryanarayan, n. 21, op. cit., p. 13.

[28] Shelton Kodikara, *Foreign Policy of Sri Lanka*, New Delhi: Chanakya Publications, 1992, p. 30.

THE 1976 AGREEMENT

India and Sri Lanka came to another agreement on the boundary in the Bay of Bengal and the Gulf of Mannar in 1976. Unlike the earlier agreement, this one did not deal with any disputed island. However, it did away with fishing rights for India in the Palk Straits. In an exchange of letters between them in March 1976, the Indian foreign secretary wrote to his Sri Lankan counterpart stating that:

> The fishing vessels and fishermen of India shall not engage in fishing in the historic waters, the territorial sea and the exclusive economic zone of Sri Lanka nor shall the fishing vessels and fishermen of Sri Lanka engage in fishing in the historic waters, territorial sea and the exclusive economic zone of India, without the express permission of Sri Lanka or India, as the case may be....[29]

Therefore, the problems of ownership of the island of Kachchativu and controversies surrounding Indian fishermen's fishing rights in and around Kachchativu were resolved once and for all by the agreements of 1974 and 1976. This position was accepted by the Government of India.

Y.B. Chavan, the then Minister of External Affairs stated in Parliament:

> Consequent to the signing of the Agreement, there was also an Exchange of Letters.... This Exchange of Letters also constitutes an Agreement between the two countries.... Both countries have agreed that after the determination of the maritime boundary, fishing vessels and fishermen of one country shall not engage in fishing in the waters of the other....[30]

While demarcating the maritime boundary with Sri Lanka, India tried a trade-off between Kachchativu and the Palk Straits. This resulted in the sacrificing of the fishermen's fishing rights in both

[29] Cited in V. Vivekanandan, 'Crossing Maritime Borders: The Problem and Solution in the Indo-Sri Lankan Context', in *Forging Unity: Coastal Communities and the Indian Ocean's Future*, ed. K.G. Kumar, Chennai: International Collective in Support of Fish Workers, 2003, p. 79.

[30] Cited in ibid.

areas. S.P. Jagota, the then Secretary, Legal and Treaties Division, said that the boundary line was 'adjusted in the Palk Bay in relation to the settlement on the question of the Island of Kachchativu'.[31] India concluded these agreements with Sri Lanka for the sake of good-neighbourly relations. This can be seen in the annual reports of the Ministry of External Affairs. They mentioned that, 'The recent agreement with Sri Lanka on the division of historic waters in the Palk Bay, which has also settled the issue of Kachchativu amicably, is an indication of India's earnestness in evolving a policy of friendship and mutual co-operation with her neighbours.'[32]

However, there was opposition to the 1974 Agreement and the transfer of ownership of the island to Sri Lanka in Parliament. A.B. Vajpayee, then Member of Parliament of the Jana Sangh criticized the Indian government for surrendering its rights by handing over Kachchativu Island. He said that the ceding of the island as another '*bhoodan* [donation of land]' and 'an assault on India's territorial integrity'.[33] Mookiah Thevar, All India Forward Bloc leader, felt that the mistake made by Nehru in handing over of Aksai Chin to China had been repeated by his daughter.[34]

The issue has continued to provoke political leaders in Tamil Nadu for decades. In 2003, the Chief Minister of Tamil Nadu, Jayalalitha stated that the unfortunate decision of 1974 and 1976 agreements, in the name of good-neighbourly relations led to the killing of about 100 fishermen and 326 getting seriously injured and 35 boats being destroyed.[35] The fact is that the Indian fishermen will not easily give up their livelihood as they have been enjoying that for centuries. In an interview, V. Suryanarayan, an academician, told one of the authors that 'the demarcation

[31] V. Suryanarayan, 'Fishing in Troubled Waters', *Hindu*, 3 October 2003.

[32] Cited in Ministry of External Affairs, *Annual Report of the Ministry of External Affairs, 1974–1975*, New Delhi: Ministry of External Affairs, 1975, p. 24.

[33] T.S. Subramanian, 'Raking Up Kachchativu: A War-Cry from Jayalalitha', *Frontline*, 21 Septmber–11 October 1991, p. 50.

[34] Ibid.

[35] 'Drop India–Sri Lanka Bridge Project', *Hindu*, 25 July 2003, p. 6.

was not done on the median line (equidistance) on Kachchativu Island'. He said that 'without historical evidence, 1974 and 1976 agreements were made by both the countries'. He felt that the 'Indian government should have taken the wishes of Tamil fishermen into consideration'.[36] He argued that 'It would be foolish to attempt the creation of a "Berlin wall" in the Palk Straits, for the simple reason that the links between the two regions cannot be severed. They are like "Siamese Twins", what afflicts one affects the other.'[37] The island is very important for Indian fishermen. They used to put up huts and stay there for a week for fishing activities.

However, in recent times Indian fishermen are being not allowed to go near the island by the Sri Lankan Navy. The Sri Lankan government argues that the island was used for illegal activities and hence it has been preventing the entry of foreign elements on Kachchativu. The Indian government never raised its voice against the Sri Lankan move. The government in New Delhi could not take the problems of the fishermen of Tamil Nadu into consideration in its policy towards Sri Lanka. It adopted a sort of accommodative attitude towards the neighbour.

This position was further elaborated when Vinod Khanna, Minister of State in the Ministry of External Affairs of India, answered a question posed in the Lok Sabha by T. T. V. Dinakaran Rajya Sabha MP, AIADMK in 2003. Dinakaran queried: (a) Had the Sri Lankan government violated the Indo-Sri Lankan Agreement on Kachchativu by curtailing the traditional rights of Indian fishermen to fish and dry the nets on the island; (b) if so, the steps taken/proposed to be taken by the government to protect the rights of Indian fishermen as provided in the agreement; (c) whether the traditional rights given to the Indian fishermen as enshrined in the agreement had been held abeyance since 1983; (d) if so, the details thereof; and (e) the manner in which the government proposed to deal with the situation. Vinod Khanna's answer was as follows:

[36] Author's interview with V. Suryanarayan, Hyderabad, 5 July 2003.

[37] Suryanarayan, n. 21, op. cit., p. 4.

No. The Indo-Sri Lanka Maritime Boundary was settled through the Agreements of 1974 and 1976. In terms of these Agreements, the island of Kachchativu lies on the Sri Lankan side of the International Boundary Line. There is no change in Government's position in this regard. The traditional rights of our fishermen regarding access to Kachchativu as provided in these agreement is for resting, drying of nets and attending the annual festival of St. Anthony. The traditional rights do not include the right to fishing in and around Kachchativu.[38]

The Indian Ministry of External Affairs believes that the question of traditional rights of Indian fishermen in Kachchativu *does not arise* (emphasis added). It is clear that the central government is not only firm about the agreement, but also does not intend to reopen negotiations on this issue with Sri Lanka.

The basic premise of the current debate is that the Tamil Nadu government and Indian fishermen in the region do not agree with the ceding of Kachchativu to Sri Lanka.[39] They believe that the disputed island was unfairly 'gifted' by Mrs Gandhi to Sri Lanka, hence the Tamil Nadu fishermen continued to enter Sri Lankan waters for fishing. It is claimed that Sri Lankan fishermen also cross the boundaries and fish in Indian waters.

Sri Lanka simply refused to reopen negotiations on the subject. Mahinda Rajapakse, former Minister of Fisheries and Aquatic Resources, who on 6 April 2004 became the Prime Minister of Sri Lanka, maintained that 'it is impossible to give it (Kachchativu) back to them as it has been recognized by the international community as an integral part of Sri Lanka since it was handed over by late Indira Gandhi'.[40]

A possible option put forth by V. Suryanarayan is to get Kachchativu Island and the adjacent seas on 'lease in perpetuity' for fishing, drying nets, and pilgrims while upholding Sri Lanka's

[38] 'Violation of Indo-Sri Lanka Agreement, Unstarred Question no. 5688, to be answered on 30.04.2003', Ministry of External Affairs, India: http://meaindia.nic.in/parliament/ls/2003/04/30lapr5688.htm

[39] For Sri Lankans, the question of ceding Kachchativu does not arise because the island is a part of Sri Lanka.

[40] 'Sri Lanka Rejects Indian State's Demand for Return of Kachchativu Island', *BBC Monitoring South Asia*, 28 May 2001.

sovereignty over the island. This is similar to that of Tin Bigha,[41] where India has sovereignty over the island and Bangladesh enjoys 'lease in perpetuity'. Under a lease in perpetuity, Tamil Nadu fishermen would be able to enjoy their traditional rights. Further, some Indian observers maintain that the Sri Lankan authorities should allow the fishermen of other coastal areas up to 5 nm in its waters. It is to be noted here that earlier, in 1976, India permitted the Sri Lankan fishermen to fish in the Wadge Bank for three years.[42]

On the other hand, a lease in perpetuity will forever prevent Sri Lankan fishermen—who are mostly Tamil—benefiting from the resources in the region, which will amount to another form of discrimination, as Tamils in the north and east of the island are waging a war on the premise of state discrimination. Moreover, leasing in perpetuity means indefinite control of India over the island with symbolic sovereignty of Sri Lanka that may, over a period of time, erode. A hostile government in India may claim control of the island of Kachchativu on the premise that its citizens have used the island for a long time. Therefore, from the point of view of Sri Lanka's national interest, leasing in perpetuity needs to be examined carefully in case Sri Lanka is willing to negotiate on the subject.

Another option discussed primarily among Indians is the issue of identity cards to Indian fishermen who opt to fish in the disputed waters. It is believed in India and Sri Lanka that the LTTE is involved in illegally smuggling war materials and goods banned in Sri Lanka. It is also believed that many Indian fishermen are involved in the lucrative trade of supplying banned items to the LTTE in the disputed waters. Therefore, talk of issuing identity

[41] Tin Bigha is the name of a strip of land measuring 178 m × 85 m in the Cooch Behar district of West Bengal. Through the 1974 and 1982 agreements between India and Bangladesh, the former gave lease in perpetuity over the land to the latter, the former has sovereignty over the area, and the Indians' right to access through the corridor remains intact. This is one of the steps to bring the people of both the countries together in amity and good-neighbourliness.

[42] Interview, n. 35 above; Suryanarayan, n. 31, op. cit., p. 10.

cards to 'genuine Indian fishermen' to fish in Sri Lankan waters raises doubts.[43]

However, in view of the historical fact that Tamil Nadu fishermen have traditionally engaged in fishing activities in and around Kachchativu, that Tamil Nadu's views were not taken into account when the agreement was signed in 1974, and of the humanitarian problems involved, both countries must take practical steps on a priority basis. One possible alternative is to allow Indian fishermen to engage in fishing activities on the western side of the disputed island while allowing the Sri Lankan fishermen to fish in the eastern region without violating the sovereignty and jurisdiction of Sri Lanka over the island of Kachchativu. It is primarily the lack of adequate catch in Indian waters that is forcing Indian fishermen to cross to Sri Lankan waters. Hence, one way of handling the issue in the long term is to take proactive steps to explore the possibilities of increasing fish resources in Indian waters and following up with the necessary actions. As H.E. Sumith Nakandala rightly told one of the authors, both the governments at the centre and at state level should take up steps to encourage acquaculture.[44] Another alternative is to restrict trawler fishing, which is causing tremendous destruction to marine resources in the region. Describing the nature and danger of trawler fishing, Suryanarayan writes:

> Compounding the situation is the unrestricted and unregulated deployment of mechanized trawlers. When prawn prices escalated in the United States and Japan in the 1960s, Norwegians introduced bottom trawling in Neendakara in Kerala to harvest prawns. The lucrative practice soon spread to other parts of the country. Bottom trawling causes irreparable damage to marine resources, because it removes everything from the seabed.

A case in point is the introduction of joint-venture fishing by foreign vessels in India that has led to a great deal of tension within Indian fishing communities. This policy, Indian fishermen

[43] S.D. Muni, 'India and Sri Lanka: Fast Forward', *Daily News*, 18 December 2003.: http://www.dailynews.lk/2003/12/18/fea01.html

[44] Author's interview with H.E. Sumith Nakandala, Deputy High Commissioner of Sri Lanka in Southern India, Chennai, 24 November 2003.

believe, will harm their profession by permanently eliminating marine resources in Indian waters. They thus organized nation-wide strikes, which led to the formation of the Murari Committee. The committee recommended suspending issue of new licences for foreign joint-venture vessels. According to Rev. Thomas Kochery, a fish harvesters' rights activist:

> In 1991 India introduced its new economic policy, which marks the beginning of a new sea fishing policy. Huge foreign vessels, working under the guise of joint venture and fees paid to the government, were given license and started coming into Indian Waters. There are some 25,000 such vessels around the world. They have depleted all oceans apart from the Indian Ocean, and are a threat to over 100 million people in developing countries who depend on fisheries for their livelihood. So this new policy was clearly going to affect Indian fisher people, and probably displace them. Ten million fisher people went on for all-India strikes. The government appointed the Murari Committee, which made 21 recommendations aimed at changing the entire deep sea fishing policy. These were accepted by the Cabinet, and since 1996, the government has stopped giving new licenses. For probably the first time, a fishing community changed the policy of globalization through protest.[45]

Fishermen in northern Sri Lanka fear that trawler fishing by Indians would eventually deplete resources in Sri Lankan waters, which would in turn have a devastating impact on the livelihood of fishing communities in this region. As claimed by Rev. Kochery, 'whether in India, the US, or Europe, small boats and small communities have no chance of survival. Everywhere the pattern is the same; only the big will survive, and the rest will be wiped out.'[46] Both countries have to take efforts to preserve existing marine resources in the Palk Bay region.

PROBLEMS OF THE FISHERMEN

Sixty per cent of the global population lives in coastal areas. Fish is an important source of protein for the poor in developing coun-

[45] Ivan Briscoe, 'The Fishermen's Firebrand Takes on the Fleets', *UNESCO Courier*, September 2000: http://www.unesco.org/courier/2000_09/uk/doss25.htm

[46] Ibid.

tries. It is also one of the key sources of employment. The final report of the Murari Committee noted that 90 per cent of fishermen live below the poverty line.[47] They therefore have to depend on fish catches wherever they are available. In their pursuit, they hardly respect maritime boundaries.[48] Indian fishermen cross the maritime boundary and enter Sri Lankan waters. Similarly, Sri Lankan fishermen cross the boundary and enter Indian and Maldives waters for fishing. Since the distance between Rameswaram and Talaimannar is about 12 km., it is not be possible to restrict the fishermen crossing neighbouring waters.

Prawns are available in abundance in the Palk Straits and particularly in Sri Lankan waters. Thus, Indian fishermen cross over to Lankan waters to catch prawns, in spite of the restrictions imposed by the Indian Navy and attacks carried out by the Sri Lankan Navy and the Sea Tigers. They argue that they do not have any other alternative than this as their survival depends on fishing in Sri Lankan waters. Similarly, the Sri Lankan fishermen cross over to the Maldives waters, where tuna fish is in abundance. Entering into others' waters and carrying out fishing activity is illegal. However, under Article 146 of the UN Law of Sea, 'measures will be taken to ensure effective protection of human life'. On the other hand, Article 73 mentions that littoral states can take measures 'including boarding, inspection, arrest and judicial proceedings to ensure compliance with the laws and regulations'.[49]

There has been an increase in the marine fish production in Tamil Nadu. Its fish production has increased from 288.95 thousand tonnes in 1991 to 330.50 thousand tonnes in 1995.[50] Tamil Nadu has a coastline of 1,000 km., the third-longest in India after the Andaman & Nicobar Islands and Gujarat.

During the civil war, the Sri Lankan Navy found it difficult to distinguish between fishing boats and boats involved in nefarious

[47] National Fishworkers Forum, *Charter of Demands 2002*, Thiruvananthapuram: National Fishworkers Forum, 2002, p. 23.

[48] Ibid.

[49] Ibid.

[50] See Ministry of Agriculture, 'Supplement on Fisheries Statistic', 1995.

activities. The Sri Lankan Navy, instead of identifying the boats engaged in illegal activities, treated all as threats to its security and used to fire at them, resulting in the killing of innocent fishermen. They followed a policy of shooting first and questioning later. The Navy argued that they suspected the sailors of being LTTE forces and they couldn't go close to them for identification for fear of attack by the LTTE cadres. Table 2.1 illustrates the number of firings and the casualties, and that the number of inci-

TABLE 2.1: INCIDENTS AT SEA DURING 1983–2000

Year	No. of Incidents	No. of Fishermen			Boats Sunk
		Killed	Missing	Injured	
1983	2			5	
1984	4	1		5	
1985	33	4		87	
1986	2			2	
1987	4	3		4	
1988	4	1		7	
1989	2			5	
1990	11	6		37	
1991	17	13		18	
1992	7			23	
1993	8	8		5	
1994	10	8		8	
1995	10	6		13	
1996	31	7	12	20	5
1997	15	13	2	11	1
1998	4	6		1	
1999	7	7		2	
2000	5	2		3	
Total	176	85	14	276	6

Source: Assistant Director of Fisheries, Rameswaram, cited in V. Vivekanandan, 'Crossing Maritime Borders: The Problem and Solution in the Indo-Sri Lankan Context', in *Forging Unity: Coastal Communities and the Indian Ocean's Future*, ed. K.G. Kumar, Chennai: International Collective in Support of Fishworkers, 2003, p. 84.

dents has decreased since 1998. This is because of the Indian Navy's persuasion not to shoot at fisherfolk without identifying them.

In the pre-1994 period the Sri Lankan Navy was very unfriendly towards Indian fishermen who strayed into Sri Lankan waters. Indian fishermen and authorities claimed that the Sri Lankan Navy entered Indian waters at times to attack fishermen and their vessels. There had been a large number of shooting incidents and attacks on Indian vessels. The Sri Lankan Navy believed that Indian fishermen were supplying fuel and other material to the LTTE in the guise of fishing in the waters between the two countries. Thus, in order to prevent supplies to the LTTE from coastal towns of Tamil Nadu and to scare them from entering Sri Lankan waters, the Sri Lankan Navy undertook extreme measures that resulted in loss of lives and livelihood of a large number of Indian fishermen. For instance, the Tamil Nadu government, in a report about the predicament of its fishermen in the disputed waters, claimed that between 1983 and 1993, there had been 372 incidents of attacks that involved firing and physical assault by the Sri Lankan Navy on Tamil Nadu fishermen. 318 boats had been attacked and 486 fishermen affected: 66 boats had been either sunk or destroyed; 244 fishermen had been attacked and injured. Over 75 fishermen have been killed; 57 fishermen have been injured in firing incidents. The Sri Lankan Navy had seized about 65 motor boats and arrested more than 200 fishermen. The Tamil Nadu government claims that in the early 1990s, the intensity and frequency of the Sri Lankan Navy's attack on Tamil Nadu fishermen had increased.[51]

Since the mid-1990s, relations between the two countries improved and there has been apparent changes in the Navy's attitude towards Indian fishermen who violated maritime rules in and around Kachchativu Island. Now the Sri Lankan Navy does not resort to extreme measures, instead simply warn the fishermen or remain inactive, claimed people in Mannar. In 2003, the Indian Coast Guard said that 'the Sri Lankan authorities make a

[51] Mukul Sharma, 'In Risky Waters', *Frontline*, vol. 16, no. 19, 11–24 September 1999: http://www.frontlineonnet.com/fl1619/16190650.htm

note of the number of the vessel and then hand them over to us as quickly as they can' because diplomatic ties between the two countries are 'healthy and progressive'.[52] Confirming this state of affairs, an Indian correspondent wrote that 'the Sri Lankan Navy, which resisted the intruders (from Tamil Nadu) from 1983 onwards, is today a silent spectator...'.[53] Furthermore, a letter addressed to the Prime Minister of Sri Lanka by the Mannar District Fishermen Cooperative Societies Union maintained that, 'Due to the unauthorized fishing by Indian fishermen, our fishermen are undergoing untold hardships for their daily living without any income. The Sri Lankan Navy officials are only checking the Sri Lankan fishermen and taking no action to stop the Indian fishermen.'[54] The Tamil Nadu fishermen find it difficult to fish freely in the troubled region partly because of the accelerated activities of the Indian Coast Guard in the region. India had also modernized its surveillance system to prevent illegal transport from either side. An Indian Ministry of External Affairs document entitled 'Indo-Sri Lanka Bilateral Relations' maintains that:

> Most of the Indian fishermen going to fish in Sri Lankan waters are from Tamil Nadu. They prefer to fish there due to greater amount of better quality of fish. They are frequently apprehended by the Sri Lankan Navy. The Government of Tamil Nadu is aware of the problem and has taken measures to discourage its fishermen from crossing the International Maritime Boundary Line (IMBL) over a long term. Given the excellent relations between India and Sri Lanka, apprehended Indian fishermen are released promptly by Sri Lanka on Indian request.[55]

The fishermen of India have many compulsions to cross over to fish in Sri Lankan waters. In 2003, a few fishermen of Tuticorin

[52] S. Vydhianathan and R.K. Radhakrishnan, 'India–Sri Lanka Accord Alone Can End Attacks on Fishermen', *Hindu*, 6 December 2003: http://www.hindu.com/2003/12/06/stories/2003120606180100.htm

[53] P.K. Balachandran, 'Fishing in Troubled Waters', *Hindustan Times*, 5 January 2004.

[54] The letter was dated 10 March 2003.

[55] Ministry of External Affairs, 'India–Sri Lankan Bilateral Relations', December 2003: http://meaindia.nic.in/foreigrelation/srilanka.htm

were arrested by the Sri Lankan Navy and put in jail. One of the authors interviewed the families of the affected. During the interview, the children of the affected families said that their mothers were responsible for their not being able to see their fathers, but the wives said that their whole family was dependent on fishing activities: they didn't have any other source of income, and since women couldn't fish, they had to depend solely on their husbands. One woman said, 'How can we run our family without earning money? My husband is the only one who is earning and if he does not go for fishing, we will starve to death.' Further, she claimed that no one, including the owner of the boat, helped them when their men were arrested. When the owner was asked for an explanation over the issue, his reaction was: 'How could I help them when I myself was not able to run my own family?' He said that he invested lakhs [one million equals 10 lakh] of rupees on his boat, and when it was confiscated, he did not have money to get it released. In one family, the son told one of the authors that he did not go to bed at night, because if his father came back, his mother would send him out again for fishing.

There is a conflict between those plying mechanized and country boats in India. The mechanized boat lobby is powerful and is hampering the country boats from fishing. There is a restriction on mechanized boats not fishing within 3 nm from the shore, whereas country boats are allowed to fish in that area. In an interview, the assistant director of the Fisheries Department of Rameswaram told one of the authors that the mechanized boats often violated the existing norms and fish in the prohibited area. There have been fights between these two groups and the Naval men were not able to sort out their differences. The fishermen who used country boats told one of the authors that they earned about Rs. 50 a day, and sometimes they did not get even this amount. However, when one of the authors met the fishermen who used mechanized boats, they said that there was not much profit in it for them. They got less than Rs. 100 daily, and from April to May (15 days) they were not allowed to fish because it was the breeding season for fish.

The Tamil Nadu government has initiated certain measures

to help the fishermen, which include, for instance: the Marine Fishermen Free Housing Scheme; National Marine Fishermen Savings-cum-Relief Scheme; Fishermen Personal Accident Group Insurance Scheme; Marine Fishermen Accident Group Insurance Scheme; Supply of Inboard/Outboard Motors to traditional fishermen.[56] However, the fishermen told one of the authors that the welfare schemes were not reaching them and they had to depend on fishing solely.

On the Indian side, the authorities are also arresting Sri Lankan fishermen who enter Indian waters. Once the fishermen are caught and brought before the authorities, it takes a long procedure to release them. Both the central and state governments are involved in the decision-making process: there are different ministries/departments, i.e. the Ministry of Home Affairs, Ministry of External Affairs, Ministry of Agriculture, and also state government departments. Unlike Sri Lanka, in India the prosecution procedure takes a longer time. Table 2.2 shows the Sri Lankan fishermen arrested by the Indian Coast Guard and the time taken to release them.

Foreign fishing vessels that are involved in illegal activities are asked to pay penalty, which is beyond the capacity of almost all the fishermen. In a few cases courts have ordered payment of a fine of Rs. 1,00,000. Apart from the penalty, they may undergo imprisonment for about six months. The Maritime Zone of India Act of 1981 (MZI) provides for imprisonment not exceeding three years, or with a fine not exceeding Rs. 15,00,000, or with both if the foreign vessels are found in any area within the territorial waters of India, or punishable with fine not exceeding Rs. 10,00,000.[57] This is against UNCLOS-III Article 73, which forbids the imprisonment of fishermen who are found poaching.[58]

The MZI grants punishment to the owner or skipper, not the crew, of any foreign fishing vessel found fishing illegally in Indian

[56] Data obtained from the Director, Fisheries Department, Tuticorin, Tamil Nadu by one of the authors.

[57] [The] Maritime Zones of India (Regulations of Fishing by Foreign Vessels), Act, 1981 (Act No. 42 of 1981), Chapter IV, no. 10.

[58] Vivekanandan, n. 29, op. cit., p. 86.

TABLE 2.2: SRI LANKAN FISHERMEN ARRESTED IN INDIA

Cr. No.	Name of Boat	Persons Arrested		Persons Released	
		No. of persons	Date	No. of persons	Date
Yr: 2000					
123	*Akhila*	8	15 June 2000	8	21 Sept. 2001
130	*Vasan Due*	5	28 June 2000	Not mentioned	
133	*Sisira*	5	6 July 2000	–	
134	*Kumar*	5	–	–	
138	*Raj Butha*	5	–	–	
171	*St. Jeradu*	4	–	–	
Yr: 2001					
5	*Nanjil*	4	15 Jan. 2001	4	24 Sept. 2001
28	*Salakumari*	6	7 Mar. 2001	6	24 Sept. 2001
29	*Vesini Putha*	5	7 Mar. 2001	5	24 Sept. 2001
35	4 boats: 1. *Kp LB-83* 2. *KAK-1 Submarines* 3. *KAK-2* " 4. *KAK-II Akesputha*	13	–	13	24 Sept. 2001
126	*Bethlehem*	5	17 Sept. 2001	A1-A43 years imprison-ment A5	A5- 9 Aug. 2002
130	–	4	9 Oct. 2001	4	22 Mar. 2002
Yr: 2002					
–	*North-west*	5	9 Aug. 2002	A2–A5 A1 & boat	18 Oct. 2002 Later
Yr: 2003					
30/13	4 boats: 1. *Dularaputha* 2. *Samanthi* 3. *Taniya* 4. *Lurdhu Math*	19	17 Mar. 2000	15 4 and boat	20 Mar. 2003 28 July 2003
3,468	*Sinjithurai*	3	4 Apr. 2003	3	–
3,431	*Kalpatiya*	6	25 Oct. 2003	3	14 Nov. 2003

Source: Data collected from Tuticorin Police Station, Tamil Nadu, 3 December 2003.

waters, and the boat and its contents can be confiscated. Till 1999, the Government of India did not prosecute foreign fishermen but released them. However, later the problem became complicated when the Ministry of Agriculture took over matters related to MZI offences.[59] Punishment against foreigners indulging in illegal fishing in India is more severe than in Sri Lanka. Though India has always taken a long time to give verdicts on those who are arrested by the Indian Navy, their lives were never at stake. Commodore R.S. Vasan (retd.), (Chennai, 5 December 2003), U. Arulanandam (Pamban, 29 November 2003), Antony Benchilas (Alliance for Release of Innocent Fishermen [ARIF], Thiruvananthapuram, 27 November 2003), and Professor Suryanarayan (Chennai, 5 December 2003) said in an interview with one of the authors that Indian fishermen were being killed by either the Sri Lankan Navy or the LTTE. However, there were similar stories heard from Sri Lankan fishermen. For instance, in the two decades of war, the Jaffna fishing community has lost more than 7,000 boats valued at about eighteen million Sri Lankan rupees, and about a hundred have been killed on the high seas.[60]

Indian fishermen enter not only the EEZ but also the territorial waters of Sri Lanka with the aim of a bigger catch. If Kachchativu is returned to India or leased in perpetuity, it would be easier still for Indian fishermen to enter Sri Lankan waters and fish illegally. In an interview, Suryanarayana told one of the authors that 60–70 per cent of the illegal fishing by Indian fishermen occurred in the area of Kachchativu Island. However, one of the authors was told by some Coast Guard personnel, whom the author met in a seminar held in Chennai in 2005,[61] that the Sri Lankan Navy did often hand over fishermen who strayed into Sri Lankan waters to the Indian Navy. They said that the Sri Lankan Navy was cooperating and the fault lay on the Indian side. When the author asked why they could not prevent illegal fishing, they

[59] Ibid.

[60] Balachandran, n. 53, op. cit.

[61] One of the authors participated in a seminar entitled Maritime Security: Emerging Trends, Department of Defence and Strategic Studies, University of Madras, 18 December 2005.

replied that they had been instructed not to punish the fishermen who were entering neighbouring waters and they could only give suggestions to them. They suggested that instead of poaching in Sri Lankan waters, the government should encourage the fishermen to fish in and around the Andaman & Nicobar Islands, where fish is in abundance.

The Indian fishermen who poach in Sri Lankan waters are mostly from Ramanathpuram region. There are about two thousand trawlers in this district, and possibly all of them poach. According to fishing communities in Mannar district, Indian trawlers enter Sri Lankan waters in thousands at a time and they can even be seen from the shore. As one fisherman pointed out, the presence of Indian vessels in Sri Lankan waters at night looks like a 'carnival at sea'.[62] Yet, many Indian authorities maintain that Indian fishermen stray into Sri Lankan waters by accident, or due to mechanical failure, or loss of direction, implying that the violations are indeed unintentional. They also maintain that these problems are only taking place adjoining the International Boundary Line (IBL), which is strongly disputed by the local fishermen in northern Sri Lanka. Nevertheless, as an Indian observer points out:

> When this fact (closeness of the IBL) is combined with the lack of proper equipment on board the Indian vessels, one may believe that this explains the inevitability of accidental border crossing by the Indian fishermen. However, such a scenario only provides a partial picture. Fishing vessels crossing over by mistake cover only a small percentage of the cases. The vast majority of crossing is intentional and involves traveling deep into Sri Lankan waters. It is an open secret that Rameswaram fishing vessels, especially trawlers, find good fishing grounds only on the Sri Lankan side and, therefore, do most of their fishing on that side.[63]

[62] The fishermen, as part of their protest campaign against Indian fishing activities in Sri Lankan waters, have produced a video clip of a large number of Indian trawlers poaching, a copy of which had been acquired by one of the researchers in this project.

[63] V. Vivekanandan, 'Crossing Maritime Boarders: The Problem and Solution in the Indo-Sri Lankan Context', conference paper, 9–13 October 2001, pp. 7–8.

Indian fishermen, however, do not hide the fact that they illegally fish in Sri Lankan waters. For instance, an Indian fisherman who had been apprehended by fishermen in Mannar in 2003 maintained that 'we crossed beyond Kachchativu, well into their waters, but that's what we have been doing for a very long time'.[64] Indian fishermen go every alternate day into Sri Lankan waters in large groups numbering five hundred to a thousand vessels at a time, as confirmed by local fishermen in Mannar.

The fishing methods used by Indian fishermen in Sri Lankan waters, especially the use of a large number of trawler has contributed to the over-exploitation of marine wealth in the Palk Bay and the Gulf of Mannar regions. Meanwhile, following the growth of the LTTE as a formidable military force, the seas adjoining the northern and eastern provinces has became a matter of concern for the Armed Forces of Sri Lanka. The LTTE not only smuggled contraband goods from Tamil Nadu, but also maintained links with Tamil Nadu even after the assassination of Rajiv Gandhi. Moreover, the Mullaitivu sea became the hub of the LTTE's activities related to supplies of arms and ammunition used to sustain the war with the Sri Lankan Armed Forces. Hence, restricting the LTTE's activities in the waters surrounding the northern and eastern provinces formed a critical part of the Sri Lankan Army's strategy. One way to achieve this goal was to restrict all activities of the local fishermen in the area, regardless of the humanitarian consequences of such an act and bring it under its total control, because the LTTE's maritime activities are most often undertaken under the cover of fishing activities. Sri Lanka, therefore, imposed restrictions on all activities related to fishing in the region. For instance, night fishing is not allowed, purchase of fuel is restricted (only 50 litre is allowed), they can fish in the deep sea (only 3.5 km. from the shores), in some areas motor boats have to be returned to the police after every use, purchase

[64] V. S. Sambandan, 'Concerns in Mannar', *Frontline*, vol. 20, no. 7, 29 March–11 April 2003: http://www.floneet.com; http://www.frontlineonnet.com/fl2007/stories/20030411002404100.htm

of spare parts for fishing boats have to be restricted by a pass system, and they cannot engage in fishing activities in areas considered to be High-Security Zones (HSZ).[65] These regulations restricted regular exploitation of the available resources in the Sri Lankan waters, which in turn lured the Indian fishermen into the Sri Lankan territories. Confirming this view, an Indian fisherman had to say, 'we have over-fished in our own waters, there is no fish catch on our side, now it is only here that we can get a profitable catch'.[66]

Although the Sri Lankan Tamil fishermen have been protesting against these fishing restrictions and Indian poaching in their waters for a long time, the relationship between the fishermen of the two countries have remained relatively peaceful, at least till ban was lifted in February 2002 by the Sri Lankan government on Sri Lankan fishermen to fish in Sri Lankan waters. This was because of their traditional links and ethnic affiliations as both are of Tamil origin. Moreover, until the mid-1990s, the LTTE got help from Tamil Nadu, and the poaching was relatively restricted, hence the Tamil fishermen in Sri Lanka wanted to preserve the traditional relationship and thus largely ignored Indian fishing activities in their waters. All this began to change towards the beginning of this century for various reasons. First, the Sri Lankan fishermen realized that massive trawler fishing could pose a threat to survival of their communities. For instance, many fishermen in Mannar maintained that they had lost their wealth and many had already given up fishing and moved to other professions in Mannar district, largely due to trawler fishing by the Indians and the military control of fishing activities. According to the president of the Fisheries Association of Pessalai, a major fishing village in Mannar, the impact could even be seen on their children, as many of them were hit by malnutrition. Some Indian fishermen took the lib-

[65] 'Strangling the Right to Work', report by the Jesuit Refugee Service: http://www.jrs.net/old/lka-spcl/strang.htm

[66] Nirupama Subramaniam, 'To Nowhere Land', *Frontline*, 20 July–2 August 2002: http://www.floneet.com, vol. 19, no. 15; http://www.frontlineonnet.com/fl1915/19150680.htm

erty of landing in some of the thinly-populated fishing villages and took advantage of the resources on the land as well, according to people in Thalaimannar.

The Cease-Fire Agreement between the Government of Sri Lanka and the LTTE in February 2002 lifted some of the restrictions on the fishing activities in the north-east that had triggered violent clashes between the poachers and fishermen, which had emerged as a major issue between India and Sri Lanka. Now, even with security clearance to fish in broader areas, Sri Lankan fishermen found that they were not free to fish in their waters as there was stiff competition from Indian fishermen.

On the other hand, Indian fishermen also did not like the changing scenario as they were used to fish in Sri Lankan waters without much competition. Therefore, at times, Indian fishermen purposely damaged the fishing boats and nets of their Sri Lankan counterparts to discourage direct competition, as claimed by fisherfolk in northern Sri Lanka.

Wanting to completely stop the Indian fishermen from poaching in the Sri Lankan waters, the Sri Lankan fishermen expected the Sri Lankan Navy to take necessary steps to prevent the incursions. However, the Navy has been adopting a soft approach, and, although it engages in some shooting and threatening, according to local fishermen in Mannar, it has never taken sufficient measures to stop the violations. This is apparent from the fact that Indian boats still enter Sri Lankan waters in the Palk Bay and the Gulf of Mannar every other day for fishing. This is why an expert called the Sri Lankan Navy 'a silent observer'.[67] The State-run *Daily News* reported that 'there are only a few cases of Indian fishermen taken into custody by the Sri Lankan Navy. However, there have been specific instances of the LTTE resorting to shooting at Indian fishermen in Sri Lankan waters to create a cause for tension between the two countries.'[68] Moreover, some very promi-

[67] Balachandran, n. 53.

[68] 'Ministry Informs Fisher Families: Do Not Become Victims of Dubious Private Organizations', *Daily News*, 12 October 2001: http://www.dailynews.lk/2001/10/12/new18.html

nent Sri Lankan ministers in the past have proclaimed that it was the LTTE and not the Sri Lankan Navy that was preventing Indian fishermen from fishing in Sri Lankan waters.

The Navy, on its part, maintains that it cannot take effective measures due to lack of resources. A naval officer in the disputed region maintained that 'even if we arrest them and seize their craft, we do not have enough space to keep them',[69] which a local fisherman termed as a lame excuse. Moreover, the small number of Indian fishermen who were arrested by the Navy had been released quite soon because of the excellent relation with the latter.[70] Sri Lankan fishermen argue that since Indian fishermen are released 'promptly', they had nothing to fear when violating the international border. This is one of the theories of Sri Lankan fishermen to explain the Navy's inaction. They believe that the Sri Lankan Navy's activities are hampered not by lack of resources but by a lack of motivation. As some foreign-policy observers point out, Indo-Sri Lankan relations are at a peak like never before. Therefore, the Sri Lankan authorities do not want to take steps against the poaching fishermen, which could upset the relationship with India.

For instance, Sri Lankan Tamil parliamentarian Selvam Adaikalanathan, who was elected from the Northern Province, in a letter addressed to the Prime Minister of Sri Lanka maintained that, 'I strongly condemn the SLN (Sri Lanka Navy) for purposely allowing Indian fishermen to fish in Sri Lankan waters as a ploy to create ill-feeling between fishermen of Mannar and India.'[71] In fact, the increasing presence of Indian fishermen and the actions of Tamil fishermen in Sri Lanka to prevent them had resulted in violent clashes, which, of course, has been creating animosity between Tamils in Tamil Nadu and Sri Lanka as their livelihood itself is dependent on fishing. The Sri Lankan government, it seems, rather than balancing the foreign-policy concerns and well-

[69] Sambandan, n. 64, op. cit.

[70] Ministry of External Affairs, 'India–Sri Lankan Bilateral Relations', December 2003: http://meaindia.nic.in/foreigrelation/srilanka.htm

[71] 'SLN Encourages Poaching by Indian Fishermen: Adaikalanathan', *Tamilnet*, 8 March 2003: Tamilnet Archives.

being of its citizens, has been adopting a soft approach. Other fishermen in Mannar maintain that the Navy has been bribed heavily by the poaching fishermen with cash and other goods from India that are not easily available in Sri Lanka.

The Sri Lankan fishermen, having failed in their complaints against the Navy, sought help from the LTTE, as they apparently have a strong naval wing, to take tangible measures against Indian fishermen. The LTTE has a very strong presence in Mannar district and other northern fishing villages and the local activities have been to a large extent controlled and coordinated by the LTTE. Moreover, the LTTE has the capacity to prevent Indian fishermen from poaching. The local fishermen in Mannar believe that the LTTE has the responsibility to address their grievances. Although the LTTE promised that they would take up this issue with the Government of Sri Lanka during the peace negotiations, it has not taken any actions to prevent the poaching Indians, claim the Sri Lankan fishermen.

Some Indian observers believe that the LTTE has been shooting at Indian fishermen. Former Indian Foreign Secretary, M.K. Rasgotra contended that India was deeply concerned about LTTE forces capturing Indian fishermen in Sri Lankan waters. He warned the LTTE that 'India is concerned over Prabhakaran capturing Indian fishermen. We ask them to avoid provocation of this kind.'[72] Nevertheless, Sri Lankan fishermen maintained that the LTTE too was not helping them. The LTTE has indeed been taking a dual approach in the recent past to improve its relations with India and constantly maintain that they do not consider India an enemy. In the press conference held in Kilinochchi in April 2002, the LTTE leader Velupillai Prabhakaran reiterated his desire to forge a new relationship with India. Therefore, apparently they do not want to disturb the Indians by taking steps to address the grievances of a small fishing community in Sri Lanka. (Details of the Sea Tigers can be seen elsewhere in the chapter.)

Hence, the frustrated Sri Lankan fishermen took the law into

[72] 'LTTE Warned Against Capturing Indian Fishermen', *Times of India*, 5 December 2004.

their hands and organized a campaign against poaching Indian fishermen that resulted in violent clashes. Their strategy was to sail to the sea in large numbers, round up the poaching fishermen and hand them over to the local police in Sri Lanka. They were trying to do what the Sri Lankan Navy was supposed to, but the conformation turned violent. In February 2003, for example, 16 Tamil Nadu fishermen and four boats were captured by fishermen in Mannar.[73] In March, an additional 23 boats and 73 fishermen were captured. After a brief detention, all of them were handed over to the local police in Sri Lanka.[74] Obviously, these attempts resulted in violent clashes as the Indian fishermen now come prepared to face any challenge from the local fishermen, and the Indian fishermen's poaching has emerged as a humanitarian issue.

It could also become a national security issue for Sri Lanka as the local fishermen are looking at the Sri Lankan government's response to this issue through ethnic lenses. They believe that the Sri Lankan government feigns ignorance only because the people involved are Tamils, the ramifications of which could lead to further polarization of ethnic sentimentalities and strengthening of the notion of discrimination among the Tamil people. For example, some of the Tamils claimed that 'only when we have self-government we will be able to safeguard our fishing resources and the lives of our fishermen'.[75] Therefore, the fishing issue is, in a sense, being used to support the Tamil nationalist arguments by the people involved. In the future, this could further undermine the national integration of Sri Lanka.

Therefore, poaching is a serious problem faced by both countries, which needs to be resolved by some sort of agreement. However, it is imperative to note that the notion of allowing poaching in each other's waters on a humanitarian plank is not feasible,

[73] '16 South Indian Fishermen Caught Fishing Illegally', *Tamilnet*, 5 February 2003.

[74] '17 Indian Fishermen Injured', *Tamilnet*, 4 March 2003.

[75] 'Only Self-Government Can Help Safeguard NE Fisheries', *Tamilnet*, 28 April 2004.

as this approach could complicate matters further and could emerge as another impediment in Indo-Lankan bilateral relations. Moreover, allowing poaching could not be to Sri Lanka's advantage. With this backdrop, the right approach is to implement the laws governing maritime borders in general and the maritime agreements reached between the two countries in the 1970s, while leaving the humanitarian issues to be handled by the respective countries and by other means without disturbing the agreed-upon arrangements.

It is noteworthy to mention here that NGOs are playing a significant role in promoting the welfare of the fishing community in India and Sri Lanka. For instance, ARIF is sincerely working for the release of fishermen from India and Sri Lanka. One of the authors met people who are working for release of the fishermen of both countries. In an interview, he was informed that they provide information to the affected families about the whereabouts of their kin. They also meet and talk to the authorities of both countries to release the fishermen. The affected fishermen in Tuticorin told one of the authors that only ARIF was concerned about their welfare, and they were being informed by ARIF about their kin's whereabouts.

Similarly, in Sri Lanka, there are a number of organizations that are involved in securing the release of arrested Indian fishermen. NGOs, trade unions, fishermen's organizations, some of them in Sri Lanka, are working for their release. In Sri Lanka, these organizations are more effective; in India, the NGOs are not that influential and effective in securing the release of Sri Lankan fishermen. Still, they are playing a significant role. The author was told by the staff of ARIF that the government often got help from them in dealing with fishermen's issues.

SRI LANKAN REFUGEES IN INDIA

The narrow stretch of water between Sri Lanka and India in the north-western border, while separating the two countries, facilitates close contact between people. This historic relationship had been strengthened by the fact that communities living on either side of the waters have a common ethnicity. Therefore, movement of people between northern Sri Lanka and the Indian state of Tamil Nadu was not something unusual. In the modern period, massive movement of people from India, particularly Tamil Nadu to Sri Lanka, took place when, in the nineteenth century, British colonial administrators decided to take labourers from India to work in the newly established tea plantations in central Sri Lanka. Migration of large numbers of Indian labourers in Sri Lanka contributed to some disturbances in the relationship between Sri Lanka and India in the immediate aftermath of Independence.

Unfortunately, however, a reverse migration from Sri Lanka to Tamil Nadu took place owing to the ethnic conflict. The genesis of the conflict between the Sinhala majority and the Tamil minority people in Sri Lanka can be traced to the early nineteenth century and by the mid-1980s the confrontation had turned into violence and civil war. However, there had been a gradual and steady escalation of confrontational politics between these two groups since Independence in 1948. Civil wars often are preceded by ethnic riots, which proved to be true in the case of Sri Lanka as there were periodic clashes between these groups in the immediate post-Independence period. Characteristically, the minority Tamils were mostly attacked and victimized in these riots. Every time, the Tamils were moved northwards, to their historic habitat, but stayed within the borders of the State. This was to undergo a major change in 1983, as a vast number of Tamils were forced to move to India following the worst ethnic riots unleashed against the Tamils in the July Riots (1983). While some of the families—mostly from the south—migrated to India by air, a large number of people (mostly from the northern region) preferred, rather illegally, to cross the Palk Straits using fishing boats. While almost all the people who moved by air settled in private households, often with their families and friends, most of the boat people settled in refugee camps specially set up by the Government of Tamil Nadu in places like Mandapam and Dhanushkodi.

Since then there was a gradual movement of Sri Lankan Tamils to Tamil Nadu due to escalating violence between the Armed Forces of Sri Lanka and the LTTE. In the 1990s, a second wave of major movement took place as a result of major military operations conducted by the warring parties. A series of assaults code-named Operation Unceasing Waves conducted by the LTTE and military operations such as Operation Sath Jaya and Jaya Sikurui forced thousands of people to seek shelter in Tamil Nadu. Currently, there are about a hundred thousand Sri Lankan Tamil refugees living in Tamil Nadu government-aided camps. The movement of refugees to and from India in violation of maritime rules remains a cause of contention between these two countries and requires greater cooperation between the two States.

In the immediate aftermath of the July Riots, sympathy among the people of Tamil Nadu for the predicament of the Sri Lankan Tamil people was extremely high. The refugees were received and treated well by the government and people of Tamil Nadu. This remained the state of affairs till the assassination of Rajiv Gandhi in Tamil Nadu in 1991. The involvement of the LTTE in the assassination created a hostile environment for refugees living in the camps. Since then, they have been living under severe restrictions and control. For instance, local and international NGOs and UN organizations such as United Nations High Commission for Refugees (UNHCR) had been banned from entering these refugee camps. Although the Indian government allowed local NGOs to engage in humanitarian activities in these camps in 1998, UNHCR is still not allowed to inspect and engage in relief work. Moreover, many refugees complained of inadequate facilities provided by the state, which could have been improved with assistance from international organizations such as UNHCR and the International Committee of the Red Cross (ICRC). The authorities who manage the camp had imposed curfew in the camp from time to time restricting many refugees from earning from outside sources, according to some of the refugees who have returned to their native places in Mannar district.

Yet, for various reasons, many refugees preferred to stay in Tamil Nadu. For instance, some of those who returned from Tamil Nadu to Sri Lanka maintained that the educational opportunities provided by the Tamil Nadu government was of much better standard than what was available in Tamil regions in Sri Lanka.[76] Moreover, for some refugees, the prospect of living in Tamil Nadu as a refugee was much better than returning to Sri Lanka as the situation in view of the war had been extremely unpredictable and some of the primary earning activities had been severely restricted in Sri Lanka. For instance, many farmers could not engage in agricultural activities as their lands are in the HSZ and fishing activities too are restricted. It is imperative to note that agriculture and fishing are two primary sources of livelihood for many economically backward people in Tamil areas in Sri Lanka. Therefore, many refugees have continued to live in refugee camps in Tamil Nadu for over a decade.

Obviously, the over-inflow of Tamil refugees had created a serious humanitarian crisis in the state of Tamil Nadu, which already had its fair share of poverty and economic impediments. Therefore, a sudden inflow of refugees in large numbers added to the economic problems of the state. Yet, many refugees claimed that the Tamil Nadu state was generous enough to receive them and even rescue them from mid-sea sandy islands and keep them in the camps. However, more than economic and welfare issues, it were the security problems that concerned the Indian authorities. The inflow of refugees and the presence of Tamil militants have created severe security issues in the state of Tamil Nadu with implications at the national level. In the early days, militants mingled with the refugees to enter the state of Tamil Nadu and made use of the camps for their activities, which culminated in the assassination of Rajiv Gandhi. Since then, the Indian authorities have been concerned that militants may continue to misuse the facilities provided to the refugees. This ultimately resulted in the placement of strict screening measures, which led to victimization of many civilians who do not have any connection with the LTTE or other paramilitary organizations.

Refugees who were suspected of having links with the Tamil

[76] Also see 'Sri Lankan Refugees in India: Hesitant to Return Refugee International': www.refugeesinternational.org/cgi-bin/ri/bulletin?bc=00713

militancy were placed in what is called special camps. Moreover, following the assassination of Rajiv Gandhi, the Tamil refugees in Tamil Nadu camps were suspected of any criminal or violent activities in the state. Hence, following violent incidents, many refugees had been rounded up and punished. For instance, in the immediate aftermath of the Rajiv Gandhi assassination, more than two thousand refugees were detained and questioned. This pattern continued even in the late 1990s, exasperating the humanitarian crisis faced by the refugees. In order to ease the problems of the refugees, Refugees International (RI), an international NGO, made the following recommendations:[77]

Government of India: (1) Permit the UNHCR and other international aid agencies access to the camps to assist the refugees. (2) Ease its restrictions on the movement of Sri Lankan refugees living in the camps.

Government of Sri Lanka: As progress towards peace is made, visit the refugee camps, ascertaining the residents' problems and concerns, and discuss with UNHCR and the Government of India, with input from the refugees, the details of repatriation to Sri Lanka, so that plans can be made on when and how to bring back the refugees safely and with dignity to their homeland.

UNHCR: (1) Continue to press the Government of India for permission to visit the camps to facilitate the return of refugees willing to go back. (2) Publish and distribute in the camps a pamphlet outlining UNHCR policy on return to Sri Lanka to ensure there was no misunderstanding by the refugees. (3) When conditions become more favourable for refugees returning to Sri Lanka, in collaboration with the Governments of Sri Lanka and India, provide an alternative means of transportation so that refugees have the option of returning by boat with all their belongings.

In collaboration with the Government of India, Sri Lanka should make plans for the permanent resettlement or relocation of those few refugees who do not wish to return to Sri Lanka.

Meanwhile, the refugee issue also had ramifications for the state of Sri Lanka. First, the trend of the LTTE exploiting Tamil Nadu as a base has been continuing primarily because of the refugee camps in Tamil Nadu. Sri Lanka has also been worried about the way the refugee issue had been used by the LTTE for propaganda purposes. Not only the refugee issue,

[77] Ibid.

but the predicaments of the internally displaced have also been exposing the vulnerabilities in the human security aspect of governance in Sri Lanka. Therefore, Sri Lanka too wants to completely curb the Tamil refugees crossing to Tamil Nadu. Hence, both governments had been engaged in discussions to prevent refugees crossing the narrow waters, and, as a result, enhanced their surveillance activities, which had obviously reduced the strength of the inflow.

Significantly, informed sources maintained that there has been no inflow of refugees to India since February 2002, instead, what was taking place was an outflow towards Sri Lanka. In other words, currently, Sri Lankan refugees in India are returning home and more have been expressing willingness to follow suit. We were able to meet and speak to some of the recently returned refugees in Mannar district. It is unfortunate that the returnees are not provided adequate assistance for resettlement, which might hinder return of more refugees. Some of the returned refugees claimed that the state was not enthusiastic about coming to their aid. Nevertheless, international agencies such as UNHCR and the local church are playing a more active role in attending to the needs of the returnees.

Sri Lanka has three categories of refugees: (1) internally displaced from Northern and Eastern Provinces, (2) those who ventured into India, and (3) those who migrated to Western countries as refugees. In relative terms, the first two categories are the most affected by the war and the most economically disadvantaged. But the Sri Lankan refugees in India are not motivated by the greener pastures and are most likely to return to Sri Lanka if the situation improves. This is why some refugees have already returned and more are willing to return since February 2002. When one of the authors met some of the refugees in Mandapam, near Pamban, the latter expressed that though they had been enjoying the facilities provided by the government, they wanted to go back to their homeland. Further, when the author asked why they wanted to go back when they were comfortable in Tamil Nadu, they said that they missed their relatives who were living in Sri Lanka and they wanted to die in their country and not in India.

The two-decade-old war showed signs of normalcy and peace when the United National Party in Sri Lanka came to power in December 2001. The new government initiated a peace process with the LTTE and as a result signed a Cease-Fire Agreement (CFA) in February 2002, which paved the way for direct negotiations aimed at conflict resolution. In spite of the difficulties and violations of the CFA, the agreement is holding and the process has not collapsed. The CFA and the subsequent peace talks raised hopes of permanent peace not only among people who live in Sri Lanka but also among the refugees who moved to India. Refugees in Mandapam were very happy about the agreement and wanted to see normalcy in their country soon.[78]

It is evident that termination of the war by peaceful means would facilitate return of large numbers of Tamil refugees from India, which would ease many of the problems created by the refugees themselves in India. Since both India and Sri Lanka wanted to stop the Sri Lankan Tamil people crossing the Palk Straits and entering India, they should, in collaboration, take steps to peacefully resolve the conflict in Sri Lanka. Nevertheless, given the history, a direct involvement by India in conflict resolution in Sri Lanka would only help to complicate the process, which has been facilitated by the Government of Norway currently. Hence, a proper strategy for India is to play a positive role in conflict resolution rather indirectly by adopting and accepting decisions reached by the parties at the negotiating table, if and when a decision is reached. Meanwhile, both countries must devise means to facilitate repatriation of refugees who have been keen on returning rather than forcing them to violate maritime rules.

THREAT FROM THE SEA TIGERS

Ever since the outbreak of civil war in Sri Lanka (1983),[79] the maritime zone between India and Sri Lanka became very turbu-

[78] Author's interview of some of the refugees at Mandapam Refugee Camp, 30 November 2003.

[79] The conflict between the state and Tamils and between Sinhalese and Tamils has been continuing for the last two decades. The main factors that have led to the

lent affecting the interests of Indian and Sri Lankan fishermen. Apart from the disturbances caused by the illegal movement of the Tamil groups, there began frequent incidents of smuggling of illicit weapons, drugs, piratical activities and assault on security forces by the Tamil guerrillas. The northern coast of Sri Lanka, Velveltiturai and Mannar district has served as the centres of these illicit activities carried out by the smugglers. On the Indian side, Tuticorin, Pattukotiai, Rameswaram, Tiruchendur, Nagapatnam have figured as the smuggling bases.

The LTTE has always depended mainly on sea-lanes for their war material and for items of civilian use. In the past these items were smuggled from south India (Tamil Nadu). According to Major General Ashok Mehta, the LTTE owned twelve ships in the names of front companies. These ships were registered with Lloyd's of London. He said that, 'Thailand was one of the bases

---

conflict are: (1) the declaration of Sinhala as the sole official language replacing English in 1956, which led to a serious reduction of opportunities for Tamils in the state services; (2) the enactment of the 1972 Constitution removed minority safeguards and gave Buddhism foremost place; (3) state-aided settlement schemes in Tamil regions changed demographic patterns.

The Tamils protested against discrimination and demanded some degree of regional autonomy and power sharing but were ignored by the Sinhalese and the government. As a result, the Tamil United Liberation Front (TULF) and the LTTE emerged as the dominant militant groups and fought for a separate State for the Tamils. Later, the LTTE became the most powerful organization and spread from the northern and eastern provinces to other parts of the country through sporadic attacks against military establishments and the Sinhalese. The Tamil youth began to fight for their rights. They trained people, procured weapons, established an army and procured their rights. Women were also actively involved in the LTTE's activities. Slowly, by 1986, they were able to control most of the areas of northern Jaffna peninsula. They demanded that the government make the Northern and Eastern Provinces of Sri Lanka an independent Tamil State.

The ethnic conflict was intensified by the anti-Tamil riots in 1977, 1981, and 1983. Of these, the 1983 riots were unforgettable because the government troops and police supported the Sinhalese who attacked Tamils. After the riots, the fights between the government and the Tamils intensified. In order to compete with the government forces, the Tamils started procuring arms from outside the country, particularly from Western countries. As the Tamil armed group became more powerful, the Sri Lankan forces took a harder line against it.

for their supply, and, through Thailand, the material is loaded and transferred to smaller boats of the LTTE around 60–70 nm off the Sri Lankan coast. Though the ships are small, they are well-armed. They are fitted with VHF communication sets, GPS, and even radars.'[80]

The LTTE has its own navy, considered to be a match for the Sri Lankan Navy. They control some of the areas in the northern part of Sri Lanka. The LTTE has emerged as the most powerful organization there and spread its activities in the Northern and Eastern Provinces and expanded in other parts of the country by carrying out attacks on military establishments, government officials, political leaders, and the Sinhalese people.[81] It has a separate women's wing. They desire to extend their supremacy over the vital sea-lanes. Tamil Nadu was considered a base for their activities. A few Indian Tamils are believed to be sympathizers of the LTTE. However, when the Sri Lankan naval authorities arrest, prosecute, and sometimes even shoot the fishermen from Tamil Nadu, the LTTE has never shown any sympathy towards them, according to one of the authors who obtained these views from the fishermen. The LTTE has also become a threat to Indian fishermen whom they confront during fishing. Sometimes, they shot at the fishermen resulting in their death. Fishermen's groups from Sri Lanka are also involved in attacks against Indian fishermen and are the 'front organizations' of the LTTE, according to some Indians.[82] Such incidents against Indian fishermen have increased in recent times. In the interviews conducted by one of the authors in different places in Ramnathpuram district, fishermen narrated their woes saying that they were being more severely punished by the LTTE rather than by the Sri Lankan Navy. The LTTE was responsible for attacking, destroying,

[80] Ibid.

[81] A. Subramanyam Raju, 'Women and Terrorism in South Asia: Some Observations', in *Terrorism in South Asia: Views from India*, ed. A. Subramanyam Raju, Singapore: Marshall Cavendish; and New Delhi: India Research Press, 2004, pp. 227–37, 328–30.

[82] 'Navy Coast Guard to Step Up Vigil', *Hindu*, 8 March 2003, p. 6.

damaging, or hijacking ships owned by the Indians, according to the latter.[83]

There is another dimension to the problem. The LTTE is demanding that the Sri Lankan government grant them the status of a *de facto* Navy. For them, access to the sea is very important to link with its overseas network.[84] In its proposal for an Interim Self-Governing Authority (ISGA), the LTTE mentioned that it 'shall have control over the marine and offshore resources of the adjacent seas and the power to regulate access thereto'. This will include the Palk Straits, where both countries share the boundary line. Some Indian observers believe that if this proposal was accepted, it could become a serious problem for India as two-thirds of the Sri Lanka sea would be under the control of the LTTE. If the LTTE exercise control over Sri Lankan seas, it will certainly pose threats to India as well, according to current thinking of the Indians. For instance, Indian Oil Corporation had been permitted by the Sri Lankan government to use oil tanks near the harbour of Trincomalee in eastern Sri Lanka for storage and trade.[85] If the LTTE's plans succeed, it may pose a threat to Indian investors. If the proposal is accepted by the Sri Lankan government, that would certainly violate the joint statement of both countries, which says, 'interim arrangement should be an integral part of the final settlement and should be in the framework of the unity and territorial integrity of Sri Lanka', according to opponents of the LTTE's proposal of an interim self-governing authority.

LAND BRIDGE BETWEEN INDIA AND SRI LANKA

Sri Lanka proposed a land bridge between Rameswaram in Tamil Nadu and Talaimannar in Sri Lanka (Map 2.1). Through this, road, rail and bridge links would be developed, which would offer

[83] See Rohan Gunaratne, 'Trends in Maritime Terrorism: The Sri Lankan Case': http://www.is.lk/is/spot/sp0316/clip8.html

[84] V.S. Sambandan, 'The LTTE's Blueprint', *Frontline*, vol. 20, no. 23, 21 November 2003, p. 14.

[85] For more detail see A. Subramanyam Raju, 'Energy Cooperation in South Asia', in *Energy Security and the Indian Ocean*, ed. Dennis Rumely and Sanjay Chaturvedi, New Delhi: South Asian Publishers, 2005, p. 200.

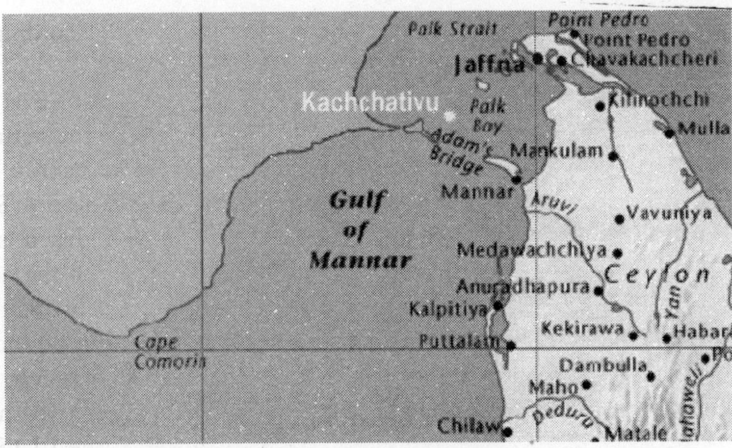

Source: http://himalmag.com/2003/october/commentary_ in.htm

Map 2.1: Proposed Land Bridge

huge economic benefits to both sides of the Palk Straits.[86] This can be one of the steps promoting cooperation between the two countries.

This bridge will facilitate improving trade between the two countries and enhance the capacity of Trincomalee port in addition to that of Colombo port. The Bureau of Investigation of Sri Lanka prepared a detailed study for the proposed bridge and estimated the construction cost as $880 million. It was reported that the depth of water does not exceed 7 m at any point. The study proposed a six-lane combination of bridges, causeways, and rail track.

Since the distance between Mannar and Dhanushkodi is about 22 km., it is difficult to construct a single bridge.[87] There should

[86] Ranil Wickremesinghe, 'Making Our People Rich', *Hindu*, 25 August 2004, p. 10.

[87] The longest bridge is the 1.6-km.-long Storbel in Denmark. See Arjuna Mahendram and Rajive Casie Chitty, 'Hanuman's Bridge: Facilitating Trade and Investment between Sri Lanka and Southern India', *South Asian Survey*, vol. 7, no. 1, January–June 2000, p. 26.

be structures which have a combination of bridges, trestles, and causeways.[88]

The bridge could become a connecting link between the national highways in south India and those in Sri Lanka. It would facilitate a continuous road and ferry link from Madurai to Trincomalee for cargo and passengers. Through this, Madurai and major cities of southern India can be connected through road and rail linkages.[89] H.E. Sumith Nakandala told one of the authors that 'the bridge would transport commodities with less time than through the ship'.

However, the Tamil Nadu government opposed the construction of a land bridge between Tamil Nadu and Sri Lanka. Chief Minister of Tamil Nadu, Jayalalitha argued that the matter must be viewed not only from an economic point of view but from the angle of security of Tamil Nadu and India.[90] She felt that the LTTE brought the 'gun culture and worse still, the horror of suicide bombing' into the peaceful state of Tamil Nadu.[91] She argued that though peace talks were being held between the LTTE and the Sri Lankan government, 'the LTTE had always found some pretext to revert to its patented brand of ugly terrorism after a quiet phase of peace negotiations'.[92] Hence, she felt that the proposed bridge would be premature and unwise.

The Tamil Nadu government's apprehensions about the security of Tamil Nadu may be unfounded. It is not difficult to prevent the activities of the LTTE and their crossing into Indian territory. It may not be difficult for the Indian security agencies to prevent LTTE guerrillas and sympathizers crossing the Sri Lankan border and entering India through a land bridge compared to crossing on sea. V. Vivekanandan, Chief Executive, South Indian

[88] The following places have such structures: Lake Ponchartain, Louisiana, USA (38.4 km.); Chesapeake Bay Bridge Tunnel, Virginia, USA (28.3 km.); King Fahd Causeway, Bahrain, KSA (25 km.); Sunshine Skyway, Florida, USA (24.5 km.). See ibid.

[89] Ibid., p. 31.

[90] *Hindu*, n. 34, op. cit.

[91] Ibid.

[92] Ibid.

Federation Societies (SIFFS), Thiruvananthapuram, told one of the authors that 'through the bridge India and Sri Lanka can improve their trade. The BAMATRICO (Bangalore–Chennai–Trincomalee–Colombo axis) corridor is proposed between South India–Sri Lanka'.

Both countries had agreed at the governmental level to construct a bridge between them. However, this proposal has yet to materialize.

SETHUSAMUDRAM CANAL PROJECT

The ruling United Progressive Alliance (UPA) Government in India approved a Rs. 2,427 crore [1 crore equals 10 million, or 100 lakh] Sethusamudram Ship Canal Project (SSCP) in June 2005. On 2 July 2005, the Indian Prime Minister, Manmohan Singh laid its foundation stone in Madurai and this project should be completed within three and a half years. The project's objective is to link Palk Bay with the Gulf of Mannar on India's east coast by building a shipping canal through Rameswaram. The canal starts from Tuticorin, extends north-east in a straight line up to Mansfield patch, south of Pamban island, then cuts through the east of the Kodandaramaswamy temple and then turns north-east to join the Bay of Bengal channel.[93] The whole project shall be within Indian waters. Since the Palk Bay is narrower and the depth is not beyond 50 m at any point, all the ships from Chennai to the west coast presently sail via Colombo harbour (Map 2.2).

The proposal is not a recent one and many similar proposals have been considered since 1860 onwards. They are as follows:

1. 1860: Commander A.O. Taylor's proposal.
2. 1861: Townsend's proposal.
3. 1863: Governor of Madras Presidency, His Excellency Sir William Denison's proposal.
4. 1871: Stoddart's proposal.
5. 1872: Harbour engineer, Robertson's proposal.

[93] http://www.Gisdevelopment.net/application/miscellaneous/misc016pf.html

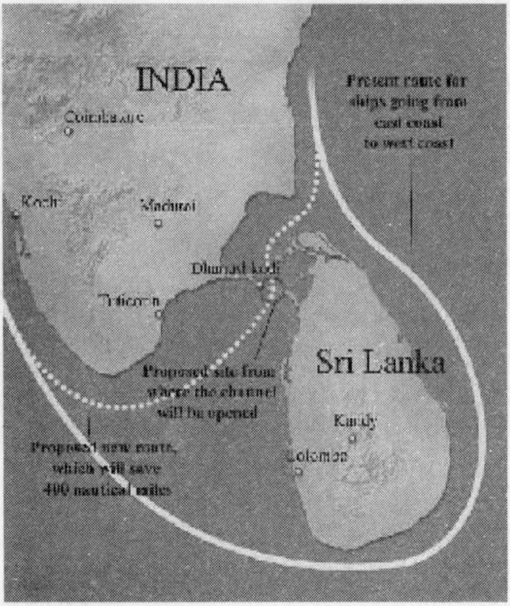

Source: Outlook, vol. 64, no. 41, 18 October 2004, p. 19.

Map 2.2: Sethusamudram Canal Project

6. 1884: Sir John's proposal for the South India Ship Canal Port and Coaling Station Ltd.
7. 1903: South Indian Railway Engineer's proposal.
8. 1922: Harbour Engineer to Government of India Sir Robert Bristow's proposal.

After India's Independence, the Government of Tamil Nadu revised the project and suggested the deepening of the Pamban canal by 20 ft to allow passage of vessels with a tonnage of less than 2,000. In 1955, an expert committee was appointed by the central government, followed by another committee in 1965 which submitted its report in May 1968. The report was revised three times. In 1980, the central government stated that though the project was viable, it was costly. From the beginning, almost all the committees recommended the construction of the canal. In

1996, the Pallavan Transport Consultancy Services revised the project with the following estimates:

1. 30′ draft: Rs. 685 crore.
2. 31′ draft: Rs. 760 crore.
3. 35′ draft: Rs. 1,200 crore.[94]

The economic analysis of different proposals gives the Internal Rate of Return (IRR) for 30′, 31′ and 35′ drafts as shown in Table 2.3.

TABLE 2.3: ECONOMIC ANALYSIS OF DIFFERENT PROPOSALS

	30′ Draft	31′ Draft	35′ Draft
With revenue and expenditure constant	9.81	8.93	5.25
With revenue and expenditure increasing 5% annually	13.96	13.10	9.06
With revenue increasing 10% and expenditure by 5%	18.36	17.54	13.19
Project starts to earn profits from the year	16.00	17.00	24.00

Source: http://www.news.tamilcandaian.com/news/2000/09/20000912_1.shtml

Earlier, the National Democratic Alliance (NDA) government had proposed the Sagar Mala Project to bring about a sea change in the Indian maritime sector. The project cost was estimated to be about Rs. 1,00,000 crore. Shatrughan Sinha, former Union Minister of Shipping, had said that the 'implementation of the Sagar Mala Project will ensure India's quantum leap into national and global connectivity'.[95] The Sethusamudram canal is identified

[94] http://www.news.tamilcanadian.com/news/2000/09/20000912_1.shtml

[95] http://www.exim-India.com/link/oldissues/jan04/html/coverstory.htm
The project's objectives are to:

- provide connectivity from ports to the hinterland;
- provide quality service comparable with international standards;
- reduce transaction costs to benefit trade and consumers;

as one of them. Karunanidhi, Dravida Munnettra Kazhagam (DMK) leader, in a letter to the then Prime Minister of India, A.B. Vajpayee, stated that, 'The Sethusamudram canal is as important as Suez canal and Panama canal in serving both economic and strategic needs.' The cost of the Sethusamudram Project was estimated at Rs. 37.46 crore in 1968, and in 1984 it was revised to Rs. 280 crore. In June 2005, the Cabinet Committee on Economic Affairs approved Rs. 2,427 crore to complete it.

Benefits

The canal will provide berthing facilities for international vessels at Tuticorin port. It will promote economic development of the backward areas of Ramanathpuram and Tirunelveli districts of Tamil Nadu; preclude circumnavigation of ships around Sri Lanka, saving fuel costs and standing charges associated with extra period of voyage and improve operation of fishing vessels.[96] The linking of the Pamban, Archankovil, and Vaippar rivers will facilitate irrigation of about 2.26 lakh acres of dry land in Virudhunagar, Tuticorin, and Tirunelveli districts; promote coastal shipping; generate employment opportunities. India can also earn foreign exchange from toll collections from international shipping, which form 50 per cent of the traffic. Tuticorin will regain its old commercial glory. It would attract foreign investment in Tuticorin district. It can be used in transporting coal from Haldia, Paradip, and Vishakapatnam ports for the thermal power plant in Tuticorin.

Though India has a 7,500 km. coastline, it does not have a continuous navigable sea-lane running within its territorial waters. Consequently, ships sailing from the east coast of India to Tuticorin

---

- promote development of inland waterways to promote an environment-friendly and cost-effective mode of transport;
- promote coastal shipping;
- promote India as a major supplier of maritime personnel;
- improve quality and quantity of Indian tonnage; and
- modernize navigational aid systems. See ibid.

[96] Interview, n. 35, op. cit.

TABLE 2.4: DISTANCES: EAST TO WEST COASTS OF INDIA

From	To	Existing Route Around Sri Lanka (nm)	Via Sethu Canal (nm)	Saving (nm)
Tuticorin	Chennai	769	335	434
Tuticorin	Vishakapatnam	1,028	652	376
Tuticorin	Kolkata	1,371	1,031	340
Kanyakumari	Kolkata	1,377	1,098	279
Kanyakumari	Vishakapatnam	1,014	719	295
Kanyakumari	Chennai	755	402	353

have to go around Sri Lanka. This canal would reduce the distance between the east and the west coasts: between Tuticorin and Chennai from 769 to 335 nm; Tuticorin to Vishakapatnam from 1,028 to 652 nm; Tuticorin to Calcutta (now Kolkata) 1,371 to 1,031 nm; Kanyakumari to Kolkata from 1,377 to 1,098 nm; Kanyakumari to Vishakapatnam 1,014 to 719 nm; and Kanyakumari to Chennai 755 to 402 nm (Table 2.4). N.K. Raghupathi, Chairman, Tuticorin Port Trust, had said that the entire sea route through this canal was only between 6 and 21 km. and it would not affect fish breeding.[97]

The SSCP will also serve as a strategic base, and reduce the response time of Indian Navy and Coast Guard vessels. It will increase defence vessels patrolling in and around the peninsula.[98]

Costs

The Government of India maintains that once the SSCP is completed, ships would save 36 hours voyage time. However, there is a view that only ships of 30′ draft can be allowed to cross the SSCP because of its narrow depth. Hence, for safety, ships would

[97] http://www.buildnova.com-News

[98] N. Ravi Kumar, 'Strategic Significance for Security', *Hindu*, 2 July 2005, p.11.

have to reduce their speed to half while crossing the SSCP. Manitham, an NGO, argues that a ship will take at least 20–4 hours to cross the SSCP. According to a retired marine engineer who worked in Tuticorin port, hardly two or three ships will cross daily.[99]

Fishermen, along with scientists, economists, environmentalists and human activists from Tamil Nadu, however, are opposing the Sethusamudram Project. The livelihood of 5 lakh fishermen in 138 fishing stations along the five coastal districts will be severely affected. There is also concern over the impact on the environment. It involves extensive dredging of the Pamban channel where coral reefs are in abundance. The dredging can lead to the depletion of fish and the destruction of marine ecology such as the coral reef.[100] The Gulf of Mannar area (10,500 sq. km.) is home to about 3,600 species of plants and animals.[101] The Global Environment Facility (GEF) of the UNDP said in its report that, 'Of the 2,200 fish species in Indian waters, 450 species (20 per cent) are found in the Gulf of Mannar, making it the single richest coastal area in the Indian subcontinent in terms of fish diversity.'[102] The National Environmental Engineering Research Institute (NEERI), Nagpur, examined the viability of the project. The NEERI report of May 2004 stated that the project was environmentally safe. It was silent on the impact of the project on the lives of fishermen. However, its report mentioned that 'there is hard strata under the soft sediment and may require blasting if the strata encountered during dredging were to be hard rock,[103] which may cause marine death'. Arulanandam, a fishermen leader in Pamban, told one of the authors that:

[99] http://www.tamilinfoservice.com/manitham/environment/sscp/ir2.htm

[100] Coral reefs are feeding and breeding grounds for various marine organisms. They act as carbon sinks by absorbing carbon dioxide and converting it into calcium carbonate. They protect the seashore from tidal erosion, providing people with living sea walls against tides, storm surges and hurricanes.

[101] S. Anand, 'India's Suez: Is it Ecocide?', *Outlook*, vol. 64, no. 41, 18 October 2004, p. 20.

[102] Ibid.

[103] Ibid.

the area is having 1 km width, 46 m feet depth and 44 km in length. The project cost would be around Rs. 1,200 crore. The area is to be widened and dug and sand to be removed. Every time they may dig up the area because sand may come from the Rameswaram shore. As a result in the long run Rameswaram will disappear.

It will not be sustainable on geomorphological grounds. R.S. Lalmohan, former Principal Scientist in the Centre for Marine Fisheries Research Institute, Mandapam, said that:

> In Adam's Bridge, the sand dune formation, like those in a desert, shift constantly. A canal will get filled within a month because of the shifting sands. Left intact, these dunes are barriers that protect the hinterland from oceanic forces. Besides, the area is prone to tsunamis (waves triggered by quakes) and cyclones every November/December. The December 1964 cyclone wiped out the entire island-town of Dhanushkodi.[104]

Sri Lanka has reservations on India's proposed project. For it, dredging of the sea might have an adverse impact on the environment and it could mean an intrusion into Sri Lankan territorial waters.[105] K.T. Rajasingham argued that there is a possibility of many islands in the west and northern coasts of Sri Lanka going under the sea. The canal may cause ports in Sri Lanka to lose more than half of its present earnings, as the project would reduce the significance of Colombo port as a hub. The Sri Lanka government appointed an inter-ministerial panel to look into the implications of the project. It feared that this project would cause heavy financial losses to Sri Lanka—ships would bypass Galle harbour and the proposed Hambantota harbour in the south which was to open in November 2004, with Colombo harbour being the worst affected. According to N.K. Raghupathy, 'Colombo will lose 70 per cent of its container traffic.'[106]

Once the construction of the canal is completed, it would break the continuous limestone formation. This would cause sudden

[104] Ibid., p. 22.

[105] P.K. Balachandran, 'Lankans Filled with Misgivings about Fernande's Dream': http://k.t.rajasingam.tripod.com/canal.htm

[106] Anand, n. 101, op. cit.

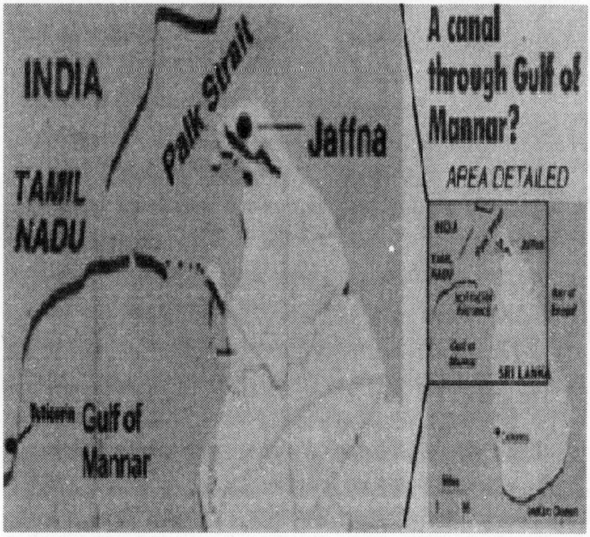

Source: http://www.asiantribune.com/show_article.php?id=25

Map 2.3: Sethusamudram Canal through the Gulf of Mannar

tilting drifts, and gravitational pull on various other violent processes.[107] Rajasingham cautioned that 85 islands off the north-west coast of Sri Lanka and a part of the Jaffna mainland would go under water if the Gulf of Mannar was dredged.[108] Also, a portion of the Jaffna peninsula could go under water (Map 2.3),[109] once

[107] Balachandran, n. 101, op. cit.

[108] Ibid.

[109] S.U. Deraniyagala maintains that the Jaffna Peninsula and the offshore islands present a monotonous flat landscape, with many of the physical features characteristic of limestone regions, such as caverns and sink-holes, brought about by the solution of the limestone along joints and fissures, as is the case with the northern coastal lowlands in general. There are large areas of blown sand, and this is especially marked on the eastern aspects of the peninsula and the islands.

According to geological survey, it became apparent that these limestone beds on which the peninsula sits, extend far beyond the island of Rameswaram, 'The present bed of Palk Strait, which separates India from Lanka, consists of Miocene limestone, suggesting that the Jaffna limestone formation is a continuous one, extending from north-western Lanka up to southern India.' See S.U. Deraniyagala, *The Prehistory of Sri Lanka*, cited in http://ktrcom.tripod.com/ktrajasingham/id27.html

Miocene-era limestone reefs are extracted and its continuity forcefully terminated.[110]

It seems that the Indian Government has taken only the economic benefits of the project into consideration, ignoring the ramifications, consequences and calamities neighbouring Sri Lanka would experience, once dredging of the sea is undertaken (Table 2.5).[111]

As mentioned elsewhere, India and Sri Lanka are signatories to the UNCLOS-III. The Indian Government should have obtained a 'no objection' from the Government of Sri Lanka as per UNCLOS. It is noteworthy to recall the provisions made in the Convention:

- Part II, Sec.: 2, Art. 6: Reefs; Art. 9: Mouths of Rivers; Art. 10: Bays.
- Part V, Art. 61: Conservation of the Living Resources; Art. 64: Highly Migratory Species.
- Art. 65 and Part VII, Sec. 2, Art. 116: Fishing Rights and Art. 120: Marine Mammals.
- Part XI, Sec. 2, Art. 145 and Art. 237: Protection of Marine Environment; Art. 146: Protecting Human Life; Art. 149 and Part XVI, Art. 303: Archaeological and Historical Objects.
- Part XIII, Sec 3, Art. 254: Rights of Neighbouring Land-Locked and Geographically Disadvantaged States.

The Sri Lankan government perceived the threat to marine life in its territorial waters along the Pamban channel.[112] It also feels that the project would reduce the importance of Sri Lankan harbours.

Sri Lanka has its the advantages of having Colombo on the international sea trade route between Europe and South-East Asia. Colombo port serves the fast-growing demand for container traf-

[110] K.T. Rajasingham, 'A Canal...and an Island...!', *Asian Tribune*, 28 August 2002: http://www.asiantribune.com/show_article.php?id=25

[111] Ibid.

[112] Syed Ali Mujtaba, 'India: Fishing for Trouble', *Himal*, vol. 16, no. 10, October 2003, p. 10.

TABLE 2.5: NAMES AND AREAS OF 85 ISLANDS ON THE WESTERN COAST DIRECTLY OPEN TO THE DANGER OF SUBMERSION (SIZE IN HECTARES IN BRACKETS)

1.	Thuruthupiddi (14)	29.	Hadujuritti (88)	57.	Saan Errunativu
2	Karuitivu (2,295)	30.	Kurjlasdduwau (38)	58.	Salliyumpiddi (1)
3.	Eluyaitivu (140)	31.	Nayinativu (422)	59.	Kalpitiyu (1,164)
4.	Partitiyu (38)	32.	Dolft (4,717)	60.	Erumutivu (90)
5.	Analaitivu (482)	33.	Kachchativu (68)	61.	Pambativu (2)
6.	Puliyamtivu (44)	34.	Irunnitivu North (422)	62.	Kilitivu (1)
7.	Kayts (640)	35.	Irunnitivu South (171)	63.	Noduntivu (10)
8.	Kuruchaditivu (5)	36.	Erumaitivu (104)	64.	Mattutivu (12)
9.	Chirutivu (28)	37.	Sinnativu (11)	65.	Ambanttativu (17)
10.	Neriyampittivu (2)	38.	Kakkativu (110)	66.	Pullupiddi (1)
11.	Kaanativu (19)	39.	Suddopiddi (20)	67.	Somativu (2)
12.	Mandativu (756)	40.	Mayatumunyi (17)	68.	Maripututivu (10)
13.	Palaitivu (181)	41.	Vidaltaltivu (40)	69.	Kappaladi (185)
14.	Avarampatitivu (5)	42.	Vaakalai (36)	70.	Taliadi (9) 15.
15.	Puvarasantivu (5)	43.	Adam Bridge (shoals)	71.	Udayarputti (42)
16.	Maativu (32)	44.	Mannar (12,646)	72.	Nenativu (78)
17.	Kannativu (14)	45.	Puliyantivu (90)	73.	Periyativu (110)
18.	Periyativu (141)	46.	Udaiyadi (108)	74.	Maativu (50)
19.	Chinnakaytivu (104)	47.	Kallianditivu (171)	75.	Karaditivu (9)
20.	Karativu (136)	48.	Achenenkulwan (92)	76.	Muttwwu (50)
21.	Kakerativu (14)	49.	Kilachatitivu (171)	77.	Maladuwa (70)
22.	Kannativu (122)	50.	Kannaditivu (60)	78.	Indrani (30)
23.	Urativu (1)	51.	Karaitivu (492)	79.	Barberyn LN (5.5)
24.	Punkudutivu (2,256)	52.	Kakativu (5)	80.	Ambalaigoda isls(1.5)
25.	Karativu (97)	53.	Ippantivu (76)	81.	Sinigama (2)
26.	Palaitivu (16)	54.	Periya Arichal (32)	82.	Waratliya (1)
27.	Kerinchativu (4)	55.	Simna Arichtal (16)	83.	Nikkaduwa Rocky Islands (1.5)
28.	Kerinchativu (4)	56.	Oddalarentivu (20)	84.	Taprobone (0.5)
				85.	Parei Duwa (1)

Source: http://www.asiantribune.com/show_article.php?=25

fic and handling transhipment in the region. It has greater facilities (Map 2.4) than any Indian port. For instance, Chennai port handles only 85,000–95,000 twenty-foot equivalent units (TEU) and Mumbai port 2,57,000 TEU, whereas Colombo port handles

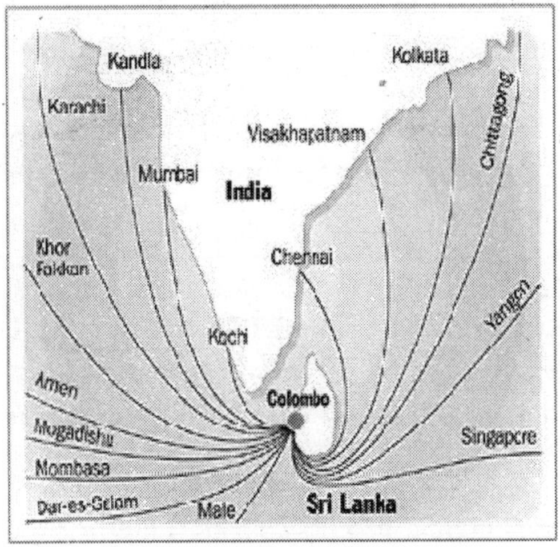

Source: U. Bopitiya, 'Using the Free Trade Agreement…', *Business World*, vol. 23, no. 43, 16–22 March 2004, p. 44.

Map 2.4: Colombo Port

4,87,000 TEU per year, and is later expected to handle 6,00,000 TEU.[113]

The LTTE also opposed the project, as it would prevent their illegal trade. The Sea Tigers are using the present shallow Palk Straits. Small boats which are being used by the Tigers will have problems once the canal is built. The movements of the Tigers will be stopped or minimized. Through this project, the Navy and Coast Guard can move around the Palk Straits to keep constant vigil on India's maritime assets.[114]

However, the Sri Lankan Government has not been taking the issue too seriously as it does not want to compromise the prevailing cordial relations with India, which is critical to counter threats from the LTTE. Sri Lanka may also be glad to accept the adverse impact of the project on the LTTE, as the Indian security

[113] http://www.thehindu businessline.com/bline/2002/11/27/stories/2002112700580900.htm

[114] V. Suryanarayan, 'Sri Lanka and India's Security', *Hindu*, 25 April 2003, p. 10.

activities will have to be increased once the canal begins to function. Increased Indian surveillance has the potential of preventing the illegal smuggling activities of the LTTE. Therefore, the general feeling among the people in Sri Lanka, specially the Tamils, is that the canal project has Sri Lankan consent, expressed rather indirectly.

Meanwhile, some of the pro-LTTE Tamil activists in the state of Tamil Nadu maintain that the new canal will not in any way undermine the interests of the LTTE. Instead, the Tamil people in northern Sri Lanka can, in fact, benefit from the project. They point out that the canal will not only enhance the viability of the southern Indian ports, but also the ports in northern Sri Lanka, for instance, Kankesanthurai port will gain new significance, expanding the economic potential of the Tamil regions. Therefore, they urge the Sri Lankan Tamils to support the Sethusamudram Canal Project. Nevertheless, Sri Lankans in general are not fully aware of the impacts of the project as private organizations are not fully equipped to undertake in-depth studies on the impact of the Sethusamudram Project on Sri Lanka and the state agencies remain ignorant. Another reason why Sri Lankans are not fully informed about the proposed project is that they are preoccupied with developments related to the civil war or the ethnic conflict.

Some recent reports suggest that Sri Lanka has taken up the Sethusamudram issue with the Indian authorities and India has agreed to discuss Sri Lankan concerns. Sri Lanka may have registered a token protest with the Indian authorities to counter the growing domestic pressure to do so. Although too late, a small number of organizations, specially institutions representing fishing communities, have raised protests against the canal project and have questioned the Sri Lankan state's attitude in this regard. It is interesting to note that the Sri Lankan authorities, particularly the Foreign Ministry, has taken steps to discuss this crucial issue after the Indians finalized the project.

However, the canal will be a significant factor in the relationship between these two States as it will have an impact on almost all the maritime issues between them. Therefore, solutions for the existing maritime issues must be examined in the backdrop of Sethusamudram canal.

One of the high officials of Sri Lanka, in an interview with one of the authors, said that the canal project could be constructed. It is to be noted that Ranil Wickremesinghe, former Prime Minister of Sri Lanka, did not oppose this project, and considered both the land bridge and the Sethusamudram canal to be compatible.[115]

Both countries should have discussed and conducted studies on the project. Though the proposed project is located in its own territorial waters, India should not ignore the neighbouring country's concerns as well as the various groups in India which have expressed their reservations.

ECONOMIC COOPERATION

Sri Lanka and India liberalized their economies in 1978 and 1991 respectively. Therefore, trade between the two has been increasing. In half a decade, the two-way trade has almost doubled. From 1998 to 2003, Sri Lanka's trade with India has increased six times, whereas New Delhi's trade with Colombo increased two times (Table 2.6). India is one of the close economic partners of Sri Lanka.

A Free Trade Agreement was signed by India and Sri Lanka in 1998 (see Appendix 5). This agreement set an example for other

TABLE 2.6: GROWTH IN BILATERAL TRADE

	1998	1999	2000	2001	2002	2003
India	539	512	600	602	835	1,093
Sri Lanka	38	49	58	72	171	245
Total	577	561	658	674	1,006	1,338

Source: Indian High Commission in Sri Lanka, cited in Rajeev Dubey, 'Bridge Over Palk Strait', *Business World*, vol. 23, no. 43, 16–22 March 2004, p. 34.

[115] Wickremesinghe, n. 86, op. cit., p. 10.

countries in the region to promote greater economic cooperation. It might have paved the way for the South Asian countries in the recently held summit in Pakistan in 2004 to have an agreement on a South Asian Free Trade Agreement (SAFTA). Half of India's investments in the SAARC countries are in Sri Lanka. India has contributed considerably to promote tourism in Sri Lanka. It was reported that tourists from India to Sri Lanka have increased from 33,932 in 2001 to 63,087 in January–September 2003.[116]

Trade

India and Sri Lanka export to each other. The main items from Sri Lanka are: spices; pulses; coconut products; graphite; natural rubber; organic chemicals; precious and semi-precious stones; artificial resins and plastic materials; pulp and paper products; furnace oil and petroleum products; and tea. From India: oil meals; fruits and vegetables; marine products; raw cotton, leather, and manufactures; drugs; pharmaceuticals; dyes; intermediaries and coal tar chemicals; toiletries; rubber manufactured products; glass; ceramics; cement; plastic and linoleum products; residual chemical and allied products; manufactures of metals, machinery and instruments; transport equipment; iron and steel; primary and semi-finished steel; cotton; and yarn fabrics.[117]

Reportedly, most of the trade between India and Sri Lanka is 'unofficial'. Trade between the two countries can be traced to time immemorial and a significant share is illicit. In the early days of Independence, contraband trade between two countries was a two-way process, with significant quantities of goods being smuggled. While the illicit trade took place by various means, smuggling by boat through the Palk Straits was one of the most prominent modes. For instance, the northern town of Velvettiturai

[116] Sanjeevan Wijewardana, 'Ties with India Cornerstone says Tyrone', *Daily Mirror*: www.dailymirror.lk/2003/10/24/news/21.asp

[117] Muttukrishna Sarvananthan, 'Contraband Trade and Unofficial Capital Transfers between Sri Lanka and India', *Economic and Political Weekly*, vol. 29, no. 30, 23 July 1994, p. 1949.

(or 'VVT') that lies on the northern coast close to India gained notoriety for smuggling activities between Sri Lanka and India and beyond.[118]

There are three major categories of goods that are smuggled to northern Sri Lanka from India by boat: arms and ammunition; consumer goods; and drugs.

Arms and Ammunition

Arms and ammunition are the prominent items smuggled from India to Sri Lanka by the LTTE. This issue has been dealt with under the section on Sea Tigers.

Consumer Goods

Goods like gold, silver, precious stones, cinnamom cardamom, cloves, imported audio cassettes/records, imported video cassette recorders, and electrical goods are smuggled from Sri Lanka to India, whereas textiles, steel products, and medicines are illegally transported from India to Sri Lanka by air.[119]

While the traditional items such as saris and sarongs still continue to figure prominently in the items smuggled to Sri Lanka from India, a large list of new items had been added to the list primarily because of the civil war in northern Sri Lanka. Following the intensification of the civil war and the increasing threat of the LTTE to the territorial integration of the Sri Lankan State, the government imposed restrictions in the LTTE-controlled areas. Goods such as fuel, cement, iron rods, batteries, chocolate, etc., were banned.[120] Obviously, the LTTE's activities were hindered by the economic embargo, which also triggered a humanitarian crisis in the LTTE-controlled areas in the Northern and Eastern Provinces.

[118] 'Sri Lanka: How a Secret Global Network Keeps Sri Lanka's Tamil Guerrilla Organization Up and Killing', *Asia Week*, 18 July 1996.

[119] Sarvananthan, n. 117, op. cit.

[120] The ban on non-military goods had been removed by the Cease-Fire Agreement signed by the Government of Sri Lanka and the LTTE in February 2002.

Characteristically, when the inflow of goods from the south was barred, the LTTE and the people looked to Tamil Nadu for supplies. Hence, the goods smuggled into Sri Lanka by boat were meant not only for the LTTE but also for the general public. For instance, a litre of diesel sold in Jaffna is ten times the original price in India. Attracted by such lucrative prospects, a large number of Tamil Nadu fishermen have been involved in smuggling of banned items, specially fuel. It is widely believed that fuel from Tamil Nadu was smuggled and sold to the LTTE through fishing boats or civilian boats. Sensing the danger of these illicit fuel transactions, the Indian authorities attempted to prevent the trade by imposing restrictions on fuel purchase by the Tamil Nadu fishermen in the Palk Bay region, which obviously did not completely prevent the trade owing to corruption within the Indian as well as Sri Lankan law-enforcing agencies. Nevertheless, the issue had been partially and indirectly addressed by the ceasefire agreement, which allowed inflow of goods from south to north in Sri Lanka at market prices.

Despite the suspension of the ferry service between Rameswaram and Talaimannar, illegal trade between the two countries has been continuing through other coastal areas such as Beruwala, Kalutara, Colombo, Wattala, Negambo, Puttalam, Kalpitiya, Mannar, Velvettiturai, Point Pedro and Mullaitivu in Sri Lanka and coastal areas of Tamil Nadu and Kerala states in India. It was reported that about eight boats of contraband trade takes place between Sri Lanka and India every day.[121] According to a survey in 1992, in each boat goods worth about Rs. 50,000 were smuggled from Sri Lanka to India. However, contraband trade by boats from India to Sri Lanka was about Rs. 10,000 worth of goods by each boat. The total trade by sea was about Rs. 4,368 million per annum and total contraband trade through sea and air was Rs. 10,911.65 million.[122] The total official trade between the two countries was Rs. 9,627 million in 1991.[123]

[121] Sarvananthan, n. 117, p. 1953.

[122] Ibid.

[123] Department of Commerce, Ministry of Trade and Commerce, Government of Sri Lanka, *Monthly Bulletin of Trade Statistics*, Jan. 1992, cited in ibid.

Both countries have to realize the fact that restrictions on trade are detrimental to their economic growth. They have to relax the restrictions on their goods by abolishing tariffs and lifting all restrictions on goods and services, which would minimize the contraband trade between the two countries.

Drugs

Drug trafficking through the Palk Straits is another major concern within the ambit of maritime cooperation between India and Sri Lanka. Mannar district has become the hub of drug smuggling into Sri Lanka from India. Drugs are purchased from Afghanistan and smuggled from Pakistan to southern states of India and then to Sri Lanka.[124] Although some observers suggest that these drugs are again smuggled to Western countries from Sri Lanka, others argue that the drugs are consumed locally.[125] The number of drug users (specially of heroin) in Sri Lanka is clear evidence that a large quantity of smuggled drugs is consumed locally, which has created severe social problems in Sri Lanka. Hence, it is imperative to pay particular attention to the drug trafficking between Sri Lanka and India. Institutions in both countries have agreed to share information about the movement of smuggled drugs and drug smugglers, which had proved to be inadequate. Enforcement of maritime responsibilities and elimination of corruption in both countries might help to restrict this social menace.

ENERGY COOPERATION

Sri Lanka has been facing power shortage. Though surrounded by water, it does not have adequate hydro potential to be exploited. Thus, Sri Lanka is looking for alternative sources to meet its demands. India and Sri Lanka had signed a free trade agree-

[124] 'Thiruvananthapuram, Maldives New Route for Smuggling', *Hindu*, 4 February 2004: http://www.hindu.com/2004/02/04/stories/2004020411100500.htm

[125] 'India, Sri Lanka to Enhance Vigil', *Hindu*, 18 November 2001.

ment in 1998. Its aim is to promote mutual trade. The former Sri Lankan Prime Minister, Ranil Wickremesinghe, while delivering a lecture at Chennai in August 2003, called for the development of a South India–Sri Lanka sub-regional single market to promote economic growth in both the countries.[126]

The proposed bridge between Rameswaram and Talaimannar would create road and rail links. The bridge would 'carry transmission lines to hook up Sri Lanka to India's Southern Region Electricity Grid with the Kudankulam nuclear power plant serving as a base load station'.[127] Both countries can cooperate in the area of power if an electric grid stretching from Nepal to Sri Lanka is established.[128]

There are about sixty Indian companies that invested 5 to 6 billion Sri Lankan rupees in natural gas and oil, shipping, education, banking, textiles, financial and service sectors in Sri Lanka.[129] It is reported that a firm Nexant, inc. carried out a study on the feasibility of a 30-km. submerged High-Voltage Direct Current (HVDC) link through the Palk Straits between the two countries for export of 500 MW power to Sri Lanka. The Ceylon Petroleum Corporation gave 100 retail outlets to Lanka IOC, a subsidiary of Indian Oil Corporation Ltd. Further, it is ready to give 150 dealers and franchise retail outlets.[130] In his paper, Wickremesinghe said, 'Together we can offer greater economies of scale and build a more competitive commercial environment. Together we have the potential to emerge as one of the most dynamic regional markets in Asia and the world.'[131]

[126] Wickremesinghe, n. 86.

[127] B.G. Verghese, 'For an Ocean Outlook', *Hindu*, 25 November 2003, p. 10.

[128] Wickremesinghe, n. 86, op. cit.

[129] 'Sri Lanka for Borderless Trade with India', *Hindu*, 10 August 2003, p. 10.

[130] Anant V. Naik, Sajal Ghosh and V. Raghuraman, *Energy Security Issues and India*, July 2003: http://www.acus.org/energy

[131] Wickremesinghe, n. 86, op. cit.

CHAPTER 3

Conclusions

There is greater need to enhance mutual cooperation between India and Sri Lanka on maritime security. Such cooperation may include measures such as joint naval patrolling, controlling of smuggling and piratical activities, and strengthening communication networks. With cooperation, both countries can improve shipbuilding, weather forecasting, prevention of pollution, and combating maritime terrorism.

Apart from such measures, there is great potential for enhancing and institutionalizing economic cooperation in the exploration and exploitation of sea resources in the Indian Ocean waters. A few steps have already been initiated by both countries to extend cooperation in some of the above areas. Yet, a more organized thrust is needed to enhance and institutionalize maritime cooperation. A research body, Indian Ocean Maritime Affairs Cooperation (IOMAC) has been established in Colombo to facilitate greater cooperation and understanding on maritime issues among the Indian Ocean States. It is a six-member body comprising Australia, Pakistan, Sri Lanka and others. Sri Lanka is very keen that India should become a member of IOMAC because it is one of the largest countries in the Indian Ocean region. The main objectives are to: (1) create awareness about the resources available in the region and their potential for the development of the states of the region; (2) provide a forum where coastal and other states could review the economic use of the Indian Ocean and its resources; and (3) adopt a strategy for enhancing national development through the integration of ocean-related activities. Through IOMAC, both countries can help each other in preventing illegal activities in the region.

India and Sri Lanka have to focus on a joint search and rescue doctrine and operations and joint development of naval projects.

They can jointly counter drug smuggling, illegal migration, and narco-terrorism. Through cooperation, both countries can improve shipbuilding, weather forecasting, prevention of pollution and combat maritime terrorism. They have to establish radio communication links between the navies of both countries for exchange of information on encroaching vessels and other incidents taking place in their waters.

Both countries should establish a joint maritime policy to tackle problems such as piracy, maritime terrorism, drug trafficking, hijacking, etc. They have to establish maritime courts in their respective states to deal with maritime crimes. They should train legal maritime experts to understand the intricacies of the issues.

It should be noted that naval cooperation between the two countries has been cordial. Every third month, there is a flag meeting between the two navies and twice a year there are 'operational meetings'. Both navies conduct patrols along the International Maritime Boundary Line (IMBL) to check illegal activities in their coastal areas. The Indian Navy has been helping the Sri Lankan government to counter the activities of the LTTE. It is very active in patrolling Indo-Sri Lankan waters. For instance, the Indian Navy captured the hijacked MV *Alondra Rainbow*, a 7,000-tonne Panama-registered vessel belonging to Japanese owners in November 1999 and apprehend the culprits. In 2000, the Indian Navy captured a clandestine shipment of weapons to north-eastern India. It was involved in helping the Sinhalese during the floods. There were floods in three rivers in southern Sri Lanka in May 2003 when 230 people were killed and 1.77 lakh people were displaced. Indian Navy OPV (Offshore Patrol Vessels) provided medical help.

The Indian and Sri Lankan governments cannot ignore the problems of Tamil Nadu when they talk about their mutual relationship. India, on its part, cannot ignore the security concerns of Sri Lanka, and vice versa. India and Sri Lanka have to come to an understanding in addressing the problems faced by fishermen in their respective countries. While the Indians want access to Sri Lankan waters, Sri Lankans think otherwise. Hence, policy makers in both countries can explore the possibilities of resolving the problem without sacrificing the interests of the fishing communities in both countries. It is a known fact that the fishermen from Tamil Nadu are violating maritime laws. Indian officials seek to reduce the incidents in Indo-Sri Lankan waters and try to prevent the entry of mechanized trawlers from the Indian side into Sri Lankan waters. The Indian government requested the Tamil Nadu government to curb the trawler owners. It has to take measures in discouraging its fishermen from crossing the IMBL, by providing alternatives for their survival. It is very important for both governments to view the fishermen's problems on humanitarian grounds, while respecting the law.

It is noteworthy to mention that the Fifth Session of the Indo-Sri Lanka Joint Commission in Colombo on 15 October 2003 stated:

> They reaffirmed the need to continue to deal in a humane and sympathetic manner with fishermen who stray inadvertently into the other's maritime zone while instituting effective measures, through enhanced surveillance to minimize such incursions. The importance of ecological and conservation aspects, in dealing with fisheries issues was also discussed. The Sri Lankan side agreed to consider the long-standing Indian proposal for licensed fishing and a Memorandum of Understanding.

It is unfair on both sides to arrest the fishermen on the ground that they are crossing over to each other's waters. It is the master/owner who is responsible for crossing the IBL. Hence, instead of arresting or interrogating the fishermen, the master should be arrested or interrogated.

On the other hand, once the canal project is concluded and the movement of commercial ships begins, there will be some sort of visible boundary between the two States. And Kachchativu Island will fall on the Sri Lankan side of the boundary making it difficult for the Indian fishermen to access the region with small boats. Only fishermen with trawlers will be able to cross the canal area and fish in the disputed region. We have elsewhere argued for a ban on trawler fishing not only in India but also in Sri Lanka, as large-vessel fishing tends to deplete—if not exterminate—maritime resources. It is imperative to note that lack of catch in the Indian side is a consequence of overexploitation by large vessels. Therefore, the canal project might remove the significance of Kachchativu for the Indian fishermen. If this is the case, then it will become a non-issue.

Nevertheless, if the Tamil Nadu fishermen continue to use the adjacent areas of Kachchativu for fishing even after the canal project is completed then it will continue to be a thorny issue, especially for the Tamil Nadu fishingfolk. Then the Indian central government, which now shows no interest in reopening the negotiations on Kachchativu, may be forced to take it up with the Sri Lankan authorities. As noted elsewhere, the Sri Lankans are not even prepared to reopen the Kachchativu issue: for them it is a closed matter. However, if the Indian central government wants to renegotiate, it will be difficult for the Sri Lankans to refuse, in spite of the fact that the demand could unsettle the existing cordial relations between the two countries, because Kachchativu has been linked to the sovereignty of Sri Lanka ever since it was conceded. Therefore, there will be enormous pressure on the Sri Lankans to stand their ground on an issue relating to its sovereignty.

This research acknowledges the humanitarian needs of the fishermen in Tamil Nadu. As a compromise solution, these fishermen could be allowed to fish in the western region of the island, leaving the eastern side for exploitation by the Sri Lankan fishermen. This would, to a certain extent, satisfy Indian fishermen without renegotiating the sovereignty of Sri Lanka over Kachchativu.

It has been argued elsewhere in this book that the Indian fishermen enter the Sri Lankan waters for a 'better catch'. They are there for an additional income, but their activities in Sri Lankan waters have developed into a survival issue for the Sri Lankan fishing communities. We have pointed out that many families in Mannar district have given up fishing as profession due to their inability in competing with the Indian trawlers in Sri Lankan waters; others are frustrated and feel helpless as the Sri Lankan Navy is not taking concrete steps to prevent poaching by Indian fishermen. This frustration also leads to violence by the Sri Lankan fishermen, forcing the Indians to use counter-violence. Therefore, immediate steps must be taken to enforce the maritime boundaries properly and effectively to prevent the illegal entry of

Indian fishermen in the EEZ of Sri Lanka. In the meantime, Sri Lanka and India can start a dialogue to address the problems of fishing communities of either side. India must understand that the Indian fishermen are entering into Sri Lankan water fundamentally due to lack of catch in their side of the waters. Therefore, systematic and long- and short-term steps must be taken to develop fishing resources in India.

It is true that the issue of Kachchativu entails a humanitarian dimension, particularly from Tamil Nadu's point of view. Hence, it requires a humanitarian approach. Nevertheless, handing over of the island to India is not practical. If India attempts to retrieve the island from Sri Lanka by taking an aggressive approach, it will deeply hurt the sentiments of the Sri Lankan State, leading to undermining of the existing good relations between them. That is precisely why the Indian Central Government currently appears to be non-committal on this issue. Lease in perpetuity is a proposal that takes into account the humanitarian needs of the Indian fishermen, at the same time preserving the sovereign rights of the Sri Lankan State over the disputed island. Meanwhile, purely from a national point of view, it might also bring some material benefit to Sri Lanka in the form of rent and so on, which Sri Lanka may receive as monetary benefit or services. Nevertheless, Sri Lankans are presently not in favour of this solution, as evident from the statements of some high-ranking government officials in Sri Lanka. India should take a conscious decision whether it wants to reopen negotiations on Kachchativu, or preserve the *status quo*. In the absence of a clear policy on this, statements and actions of regional leaders might adversely affect the existing good relations.

It has been argued that it is because of the high-intensity violence emanating from the ethno-political war, refugees are being created in Sri Lanka, who illegally cross the Palk Straits and enter Tamil Nadu. Nevertheless, since the conflicting parties in Sri Lanka have entered into a cease-fire agreement, and since the agreement is holding amidst a number of skirmishes, a large number of refugees in India have returned to Sri Lanka, yet again illegally. Many more are willing to return, but are stranded in India due to bureaucratic hurdles and security screening procedures of the Indian agencies. Therefore, many people are attempting to illegally return to their motherland, sometimes sacrificing their lives. The Sri Lankan Navy is extremely alert in detaining these illegally returning refugees, resulting in the detention of many.

A number of steps could be taken by India, Sri Lanka and international agencies to address the issues of these refugees, as follows:

1. The Tamil Nadu state could speed up the processing of applications of refugees to return and allow the international humanitarian agencies to assist the refugees who are not willing to return to Sri Lanka immediately.
2. International humanitarian agencies such as UNHCR could be allowed to facilitate legal and decent return of these refugees to their places of origin.
3. The Sri Lankan State could facilitate their return by providing necessary facilities for resettlement and legal assistance to reintegrate them into the Sri Lankan society.

These are some of the immediate steps that could be taken to address the issues of the refugees. Nevertheless, the fundamental need is to prevent the inflow of refugees from Sri Lanka to India. This can be done only by terminating the war between the Sri Lankan State and the LTTE and resolving the ethno-political conflict. It is well understood in Sri Lanka that a solution to the ethnic conflict is not possible without the blessings of the Indians. Therefore, India could, from outside the process, support the ongoing efforts at conflict resolution in Sri Lanka.

At governmental level, India and Sri Lanka have been maintaining cordial relations. Both countries can understand each other's sentiments and compulsions. They recognize the importance of each other. One could say that India's relations with Sri Lanka are much better than its relations with any other country in South Asia. Their mutual understanding and their trade agreement in 1998 (see Appendix 5) probably became one of the factors making the South Asian countries to sign the SAFTA in January 2004 at the Islamabad SAARC Summit.

After the FTA was signed by India and Sri Lanka, illegal trade between them has been drastically reduced, because the items are freely available on both sides. However, the illegal trade would be further reduced once India and Sri Lanka signed the Comprehensive Economic Partnership Agreement (CEPA). In other words, both the governments should realize the fact that unless there is a free flow of trade between the two countries, it would be difficult to eliminate contraband trade.

One of the ways to prevent illegal trade between the two territories is to strengthen the Coast Guard activities of both States in the border regions and enhance the surveillance tools available. This could prevent illegal trade activities and also illegal fishing activities. It was noted elsewhere that, to a certain extent, illegal trade and similar dealings are facilitated by the Indian fishermen in Sri Lanka. Therefore, enhanced surveillance could prevent illegal fishing activities of the Indians in Sri Lanka as well. This will also have a preventive effect on drug trafficking from India to Sri Lanka and vice versa.

India and Sri Lanka have to promote a dialogue between their civil societies. They can create a better future for their people through mutual cooperation. They have to address the common and similar problems being faced by them by sharing their experiences, collaborative analysis of the current situation, and assessing future scenarios and prospects for human development. There has to be networking among fishermen of both countries by bringing them onto a common platform, where they can discuss their problems, share their experiences and exchange ideas, which may, in the long run bring about unity among them. India and Sri Lanka can have a common maritime law, so that fishermen can be released without much delay in case they enter the other's waters.

By way of concluding, it is noteworthy to recall what Ranil Wickremesinghe, Prime Minister of Sri Lanka, had said (*Hindu*, 25 August 2003): 'All it requires is the imagination, the leadership and the commitment to shake off the shackles of the past, bring peace to this part of the region to make our people rich.'

APPENDIX 1

Delimitation of the Gulf of Mannar and Palk Strait, 25th October 1921

Copy of the letter from C.W.E. Cotton, Esq., CYE, ICS, dated the 25th October 1921.

I have the honour to submit herewith a copy of the report of the delegates of the Government of Madras and Ceylon on the delimitation of Palk Strait, and the Gulf of Mannar which was signed this morning. The delegation met at Council Chamber, Ceylon, at 2.30 p.m. yesterday, and, after a little preliminary fencing, the Hon'ble Mr Horsburgh on behalf of the Ceylon delegation proposed for our consideration that the delimitation should follow the median line, subject to an incursion beyond that line so as to include the islet of Kachchativu and three miles to the westward, Mr Horsburgh maintained that this islet belongs to Ceylon and quoted from correspondence with the Government of India in which possession was definitely claimed, and, it was to be inferred, acquiesced in. We were entirely unprepared for this and had received no instructions either to consent or admit such a claim. For all we know, the Madras Government or the Government of India is in possession of documentary evidence which conclusively rebuts Mr Horsburgh's contentions. Mr Leach informed the meeting that the Rajah of Ramand asserts that Kachchativu is within his Zamindari, that it forms part of the original area on which Poishoush was calculated, that it had been leased to the father of the present lessee by a former Setupati and that he is receiving rent therefrom, but Mr Horsburgh retorted that if the territorial claim of the Ceylon Government to this islet was disputed by us, the conference must dissolve. It may be recalled that at the preliminary meeting held at Fort St. George the line proposed to be adopted by us ran only about a mile to the eastward of Kachchativu, which indicated that its neighbourhood was not considered of any importance from a fisheries point of view and having again obtained assurance from Mr Hornell on this point, we unanimously decided that the delimitation of the new jurisdictions for fishing purposes could be decided independently of the question of territoriality. The delimitation line was accordingly fixed, with our concurrence 3 miles west of Kachchativu and the Ceylon representatives thereupon agreed to a more orderly alignment south of the island than they had originally proposed, so that important chank beds in that area should fall entirely within the Madras sphere of influence. The line where it crosses Adam's Bridge was fixed exactly half way between Dhanushkodi and Talaimannar, an arrangement agreeable to both parties in view of the contingency that the cost of a bridge along this natural causeway is likely to be appointed according to such division. The remainder of the line was accepted without discussion and a draft report was then prepared and agreed to. To this report, it will be seen that we have added a rider, so as not to prejudice any territorial claim which the Government of Madras or the Government of India may wish to prefer in respect of this islet of Kachchativu, but I am to explain that we consider that even if such a claim should be pressed and prevail, there is no necessity, so far as the valuable pearl and chank fisheries are concerned for any consequential modification being demanded of the delimitation line which the Conference has unanimously approved. We are inclined to regard the Ceylon claim to this islet as sentimental rather than practical, and consider that the advantage gained elsewhere more than compensate the Government of Madras for the loss of any fishing rights in its immediate neighbourhood. The other members of the delegation have seen and concur in this report.

After some discussion, it was unanimously agreed that the line of delimitation of Palk's Strait and the Gulf of Mannar between the Government of India and the Government of Ceylon should run as follows:

Starting from a point in Palk's Strait.

A.	Long.	80° 3′ E.
	Lat.	10° 05′ N.
	To a point B.	
B.	Long.	79° 35′ E.
	Lat.	9° 57′ N.
	To a point C.	
C.	Long.	79° 21′ E.

	Lat.	9° 38′ N.
	To a point D.	
D.	Long.	79° 32′ E.
	Lat.	9° 13′ N.
	To a point E.	
E.	Long.	79° 32′ E.
	Lat.	9° 6' N.

On Adam's Bridge, and hence in the Gulf of Mannar by a line due S.W. true from

Long.	79° 32′ E.
Lat.	9° 6′ N.

To the parallel of Lat. S.N.

C.W.E. Cotton	:	Representing the Government of Madras
G.H. Finnis	:	
James Hornell	:	
A.G. Leach	:	

B.Horsburgh	:	Representing the Government of Ceylon.
B.Constantine	:	
W.C.S. Inglies	:	
Dr. J. Pearson	:	

The above is signed by us, representative of the Government of Madras, without prejudice to any territorial claim which may be made by the Government of India to the island of Kachchativu.

C.W.E. Cotton
G.H. Finnis
James Hornell
A.G. Leach

Colombo, 26th October 1921

APPENDIX 2

Agreement between Sri Lanka and India on the Boundary in Historic Waters between the two Countries and Related Matters, 26 and 28 June 1974

The Government of the Republic of Sri Lanka and the Government of the Republic of India,

Desiring to determine the boundary line in the historic waters between Sri Lanka and India and to settle the related matters in a manner which is fair and equitable to both sides,

Having examined the entire question from all angles and taken into account the historical and other evidence and legal aspects thereof,

Have agreed as follows:

Article 1

The boundary between Sri Lanka and India in the waters from Palk Strait to Adam's Bridge shall be arcs of Great Circles between the following positions, in the sequence given below, defined by latitude and longitude:

Position 1: 10° 05′ North, 80° 03′ East
Position 2: 09° 57′ North, 79° 35′ East
Position 3: 09° 40.15′ North, 79° 22.60′ East
Position 4: 09° 21.80' North, 79° 30.70′ East
Position 5: 09° 13′ North, 79° 32′ East
Position 6: 09° 06′ North, 79° 32′ East

Article 2

The co-ordinates of the positions specified in Article 1 are geographical co-ordinates and the straight lines connecting them are indicated in the chart annexed hereto which has been signed by the surveyors authorized by the two Governments, respectively.

Article 3

The actual location of the aforementioned positions at sea and on the sea-bed shall be determined by a method to be mutually agreed upon by the surveyors authorized for the purpose by the two Governments, respectively.

Article 4

Each country shall have sovereignty and exclusive jurisdiction and control over the waters, the islands, the continental shelf and the subsoil thereof, falling on its own side of the aforesaid boundary.

Article 5

Subject to the foregoing, Indian fishermen and pilgrims will enjoy access to visit Kachchativu as hitherto, and will not be required by Sri Lanka to obtain travel documents or visas for these purposes.

Article 6

The vessels of Sri Lanka and India will enjoy in each other's waters such rights as they have traditionally enjoyed therein.

Article 7

If any single geological petroleum or natural gas structure or field, or any single geological structure or field of any other mineral deposit, including sand or gravel, extends across the boundary referred to in Article 1 and the part of such structure or field which is situated on one side of the boundary is exploited, in whole or in part, from the other side of the boundary, the two countries shall seek to reach agreement as to the manner in which the structure or field shall be most effectively exploited and the manner in which the proceeds deriving there from shall be apportioned.

Article 8

This Agreement shall be subject to ratification. It shall enter into force on the date of exchange of the instruments of ratification which will take place as soon as possible.

For the Government of the
Republic of India

Sd/-Indira Gandhi

For the Government of the
Republic of Sri Lanka

Sd/- Sirimavo R.D. Bandaranaike

APPENDIX 3

Agreement between Sri Lanka and India on the Maritime Boundary between the two Countries in the Gulf of Mannar and the Bay of Bengal and Related Matters, 23 March 1976

23 March 1976

The Government of the Republic of Sri Lanka and the Government of the Republic of India,

Recalling that the boundary in the Palk Strait has been settled by the Agreement between the Republic of Sri Lanka and the Republic of India on the Boundary in Historic Waters between the Two Countries and Related Matters, signed on 26/28 June, 1974,

And desiring to extend that boundary by determining the maritime boundary between the two countries in the Gulf of Mannar and the Bay of Bengal,

Have agreed as follows:

Article 1

The maritime boundary between Sri Lanka and India in the Gulf of Mannar shall be arcs of great circles between the following positions, in the sequence given below, defined by latitude and longitude:

Position 1 m: 09° 06.0′ N 79° 32.0′ E
Position 2 m: 09° 00.0′ N 79° 31.3′ E
Position 3 m: 08° 53.8′ N 79° 29.3′ E
Position 4 m: 08° 40.0′ N 79° 18.2′ N
Position 5 m: 08° 37.2′ N 79° 13.0′ E
Position 6 m: 08° 31.2′ N 79° 04.7′ E
Position 7 m: 08° 22.2′ N 78° 55.4′ E
Position 8 m: 08° 12.2′ N 78° 53.7′ E
Position 9 m: 07° 35.3′ N 78° 45.7′ E

Position 10 m: 07° 21.0′ N 78° 38.8′ E
Position 11 m: 06° 30.8′ N 78° 12.2′ E
Position 12 m: 05° 53.9′ N 77° 50.7′ E
Position 13 m: 05° 00.0′ N 77° 10.6′ E

The extension of the boundary beyond position 13m will be done subsequently.

Article 2

The maritime boundary between Sri Lanka and India in the Bay of Bengal shall be arcs of great circles between the following positions, in the sequence given below, defined by latitude and longitude:

Position 1 b: 10° 05.0′ N 80° 03.0′ E
Position 1 ba: 10° 05.8′ N 80° 05.0′ E
Position 1 bb: 10° 08.4′ N 80° 09.5′ E
Position 2 b: 10° 33.0′ N 80° 46.0′ E
Position 3 b: 10° 41.7′ N 81° 02.5′ E
Position 4 b: 11° 02.7′ N 81° 56.0′ E
Position 5 b: 11° 16.0′ N 82° 24.4′ E
Position 6 b: 11° 26.6′ N 83° 22.0′ E

Article 3

The co-ordinates of the positions specified in Articles 1 and 2 are geographical co-ordinates and the straight lines connecting them are indicated in the chart annexed hereto, which has been signed by the surveyors duly authorised by the two Governments respectively.

Article 4

The actual location at sea and on the sea-bed of the positions specified in Articles 1 and 2 shall be determined by a method to be mutually agreed upon by the surveyors authorised for the purpose by the two Governments, respectively.

Article 5

(1) Each Party shall have sovereignty over the historic waters and territorial sea, as well as over the islands, falling on its side of the aforesaid boundary.

(2) Each Party shall have sovereign rights and exclusive jurisdiction over the continental shelf and the exclusive economic zone as well as over their resources, whether living or non-living, falling on its side of the aforesaid boundary.

(3) Each Party shall respect rights of navigation through its territorial sea and exclusive economic zone in accordance with its laws and regulations and the rules of international law.

Article 6

If any single geological petroleum or natural gas structure or field, or any single geological structure or field of any mineral deposit, including sand or gravel, extends across the boundary referred to in Articles 1 and 2 and the part of such structure or field which is situated on one side of the boundary is exploited, in whole or in part, from the other side of the boundary, the two countries shall seek to reach agreement as to the manner in which the structure or field shall be most effectively exploited and the manner in which the proceeds deriving there from shall be apportioned.

Article 7

The Agreement shall be subject to ratification. It shall enter into force on the date of exchange of instruments of ratification, which shall take place as soon as possible.

New Delhi, 23rd March 1976

APPENDIX 4

Supplementary Agreement between Sri Lanka and India on the Extension of the Maritime Boundary between the two Countries in the Gulf of Mannar from Position 13m to the Trijunction Point between Sri Lanka, India and Maldives (Point T), 22 November 1976

The Government of the Republic of Sri Lanka and the Government of the Republic of India

Recalling the Agreement between Sri Lanka and India on the Maritime Boundary between the two countries in the Gulf of Mannar and the Bay of Bengal and related matters, which was signed in March 1976 (a copy of which is annexed hereto marked Annex I), and which, in Article 1, provides that 'the extension of the boundary beyond position 13m will be done subsequently',

Recalling the Agreement between Sri Lanka, India and Maldives concerning the determination of the trijunction point between the three countries in the Gulf of Mannar, which was signed by the representatives of the three Governments in July 1976 (copy of which is annexed hereto marked Annex II),

And desiring to extend the maritime boundary between Sri Lanka and India in the Gulf of Mannar from position 13m to the trijunction point (Point T),

Have agreed as follows:

Article 1

The maritime boundary between Sri Lanka and India in the Gulf of Mannar beyond position 13m, defined in the Maritime Boundary Agreement of March 1976 (Annex I), up to the trijunction point (Point T) defined in the trilateral agreement of July 1976 (Annex II) shall be arcs of great circles between the following positions, defined by latitude and longitude:

Position 13m: 05° 00.0′ N 77° 10.6′ E
Point T: 04° 47.04′ N 77° 01.40′ E

Article 2

The provisions of Article III to Article VII of the Maritime Boundary Agreement of March 1976 (Annex I) shall apply, mutatis mutandis, to this Agreement, as if this Agreement were supplementary to and an integral part of that Agreement.

Colombo, 22nd November 1976

APPENDIX 5

Free Trade Agreement between the Republic of India and the Democratic Socialist Republic of Sri Lanka, 1998

PREAMBLE

The Government of the Republic of India and the Government of the Democratic Socialist Republic of Sri Lanka (hereinafter referred to as the 'Contracting Parties').

CONSIDERING that the expansion of their domestic markets, through economic integration, is a vital prerequisite for accelerating their processes of economic development.

BEARING in mind the desire to promote mutually beneficial bilateral trade.

CONVINCED of the need to establish and promote free trade arrangements for strengthening intra-regional economic cooperation and the development of national economies.

FURTHER RECOGNIZING that progressive reductions and elimination of obstacles to bilateral trade through a bilateral free trade agreement (hereinafter referred to as 'The Agreement') would contribute to the expansion of world trade.

HAVE agreed as follows:

Article I

OBJECTIVES

1. The Contracting Parties shall establish a Free Trade Area in accordance with the provisions of this Agreement and in conformity with relevant provisions of the General Agreement on Tariff and Trade, 1994.
2. The objectives of this Agreement are:
   (i) To promote through the expansion of trade the harmonious development of the economic relations between India and Sri Lanka.

(ii) To provide fair conditions of competition for trade between India and Sri Lanka.
(iii) In the implementation of this Agreement the Contracting Parties shall pay due regard to the principle of reciprocity.
(iv) To contribute in this way, by the removal of barriers to trade, to the harmonious development and expansion of world trade.

Article II

DEFINITIONS

For the purpose of this agreement:

1. 'Tariffs' means basic customs duties included in the national schedules of the Contracting Parties.
2. 'Products' means all products including manufactures and commodities in their raw, semi-processed and processed forms.
3. 'Preferential Treatment' means any concession or privilege granted under this Agreement by a Contracting Party through the elimination of tariffs on the movement of goods.
4. 'The Committee' means the Joint Committee referred to in Article XI.
5. 'Serious Injury' means significant damage to domestic producers, of like or similar products resulting from a substantial increase of preferential imports in situations which cause substantial losses in terms of earnings, production or employment unsustainable in the short term. The examination of the impact on the domestic industry concerned shall also include an evaluation of other relevant economic factors and indices having a bearing on the state of the domestic industry of that product.
6. 'Threat of serious injury' means a situation in which a substantial increase of preferential imports is of a nature so as to cause 'Serious injury' to domestic producers, and that such injury, although not yet existing is clearly imminent. A determination of threat of serious injury shall be based on facts and not on more allegation, conjecture, or remote or hypothetical possibility.
7. 'Critical circumstances' means the emergence of an exceptional situation where massive preferential imports are causing or threatening to cause 'serious injury' difficult to repair and which calls for immediate action.

Article III

ELIMINATION OF TARIFFS

The Contracting Parties hereby agree to establish a Free Trade Area for the purpose of free movement of goods between their countries through elimination of tariffs on the movement of goods in accordance with the provisions of Annexures A and B which shall form an integral part of this Agreement.

Article IV

GENERAL EXCEPTIONS

Nothing in this Agreement shall prevent any Contracting Party from taking action and adopting measures, which it considers necessary for the protection of its national security, the protection of public morals, the protection of human, animal or plant life and health, and the protection of articles of artistic, historic and archaeological value, as is provided for in Articles XX and XXI of the General Agreement on Tariff and Trade, 1994.

Article V

NATIONAL TREATMENT

The Contracting Parties affirm their commitment to the principles enshrined in Article III of GATT 1994.

Article VI

STATE TRADING ENTERPRISES

1. Nothing in this Agreement shall be construed to prevent a Contracting Party from maintaining or establishing a state trading enterprise as understood in Article XVII of General Agreement on Tariff and Trade, 1994.
2. Each Contracting Party shall ensure that any state enterprise that it maintains or establishes acts in a manner that is not inconsistent with the obligations of the Contracting Parties, under this Agreement and accords non-discriminatory treatment in the import from and export to the other Contracting Party.

Article VII

RULES OF ORIGIN

1. Products covered by the provisions of this Agreement shall be eligible for preferential treatment provided they satisfy the Rules of Origin as set out in Annexure C to this Agreement which shall form an integral part of this Agreement.
2. For the development of specific sectors of the industry of either Contracting Party, lower value addition norms for the products manufactured or produced by those sectors may be considered through mutual negotiations.

Article VIII

SAFEGUARD MEASURES

1. If any product, which is the subject of preferential treatment under this Agreement, is imported into the territory of a Contracting Party in such a manner or in such quantities as to cause or threaten to cause, serious injury in the importing Contracting Party, the importing Contracting Party may, with prior consultations except in critical circumstances, suspend provisionally without discrimination the preferential treatment accorded under the Agreement.
2. When action has been taken by either Contracting Party in terms of paragraph 1 of this Article, it shall simultaneously notify the other Contracting Party and the Joint Committee established in terms of Article XI. The Committee shall enter into consultations with the concerned Contracting Party and endeavor to reach mutually acceptable agreement to remedy the situation. Should the consultations in the Committee fail to resolve the issue within sixty days, the party affected by such action shall have the right to withdraw the preferential treatment.

Article IX

DOMESTIC LEGISLATION

The Contracting Parties shall be free to apply their domestic legislation to restrict imports, in cases where prices are influenced by unfair trade practices like subsidies or dumping. Subsidies and dumping shall be understood to have the same meaning as in the General Agreement on Tariff and Trade, 1994 and the relevant WTO Agreements.

Article X

BALANCE OF PAYMENT MEASURES

1. Notwithstanding the provisions of this Agreement, any Contracting Party facing balance of payments difficulties may suspend provisionally the preferential treatment as to the quantity and value of merchandise permitted to be imported under the Agreement. When such action has taken place, the Contracting Party, which initiates such action shall simultaneously notify the other Contracting Party.
2. Any Contracting Party, which takes action according to paragraph 1 of this Article, shall afford, upon request from the other Contracting Party, adequate opportunities for consultations with a view to preserving the stability of the preferential treatment provided under this Agreement.

Article XI

JOINT COMMITTEE

1. A Joint Committee shall be established at Ministerial level. The Committee shall meet at least once a year to review the progress made in the implementation of this Agreement and to ensure that benefits of trade expansion emanating from this Agreement accrue to both Contracting Parties equitably. The Committee may set up Sub-Committees and/or Working Groups as considered necessary.
2. In order to facilitate cooperation in customs matters, the Contracting Parties agree to establish a Working Group on customs related issues including harmonization of tariff headings. The Working Group shall meet as often as required and shall report to the Committee on its deliberations.
3. The Committee shall accord adequate opportunities for consultation on representations made by any Contracting Party with respect to any matter affecting the implementation of the Agreement. The Committee shall adopt appropriate measures for settling any matter arising from such representations within 6 months of the representation being made. Each Contracting Party shall implement such measures immediately.

4. The Committee shall nominate one apex chamber of trade and industry in each country as the nodal chamber to represent the views of the trade and industry on matters relating to this Agreement.

Article XII

CONSULTATIONS

1. Each Contracting Party shall accord sympathetic consideration to and shall afford adequate opportunity for, consultations regarding such representations as may be made by the other Contracting Party with respect to any matter affecting the operation of this Agreement.
2. The Committee may meet at the request of a Contracting Party to consider any matter for which it has not been possible to find a satisfactory solution through consultations under paragraph 1 above.

Article XIII

SETTLEMENT OF DISPUTES

1. Any dispute that may arise between commercial entities of the Contracting Parties shall be referred for amicable settlement to the nodal apex chambers. Such references shall, as far as possible, be settled through mutual consultations by the Chambers. In the event of an amicable solution not being found, the matter shall be referred to an Arbitral Tribunal for a binding decision. The Tribunal shall be constituted the Joint Committee in consultation with the relevant Arbitration Bodies in the two countries.
2. Any dispute between the Contracting Parties regarding the interpretation and application of the provisions of this Agreement or any instrument adopted within its framework shall be amicably settled through negotiations failing which a notification may be made to the Committee by any one of the Contracting Parties.

Article XIV

DURATION AND TERMINATION OF AGREEMENT

This Agreement shall remain in force until either Contracting Party terminates this Agreement by giving six months written notice to the other of its intention to terminate the Agreement.

Article XV

AMENDMENTS

The Agreement may be modified or amended through mutual agreement of the Contracting Parties. Proposals for such modifications or amendments shall be submitted to the Joint Committee and upon acceptance by the Joint Committee, shall be approved in accordance with the applicable legal procedures of each Contracting Party. Such modifications or amendments shall become effective when confirmed through an exchange of diplomatic notes and shall constitute an integral part of the Agreement. Provided however that in emergency situations, proposals for modifications may be considered by the Contracting Parties and if agreed, given effect to through an exchange of diplomatic notes.

Article XVI

ANNEXURES TO BE FINALIZED

Annexure D(i) and D(ii) (Negative Lists of India and Sri Lanka respectively), E (Items on which India has undertaken to give 100% tariff concession on coming into force of the Agreement) and F (Items on which Sri Lanka has undertaken to give 100% tariff concession on the coming into force of the Agreement) shall be finalized within a period of 60 days of the signing of this Agreement. All the Annexures shall form an integral part of the Agreement.

Article XVII

ENTRY INTO FORCE

The Agreement shall enter into force on the thirtieth day after the Contracting Parties hereto have notified each other that their respective constitutional requirements and procedures have been completed.

In witness where of the undersigned, duly authorised thereto by their respective Governments, have signed this Agreement.

Done in duplicate at New Delhi this 28th day of December 1998 in two originals in the English language.

Sd/-
For the Government of the Republic of India

Sd/-
For the Government of the Democratic Socialist Republic of Sri Lanka

ANNEXURE 'A'

CONCESSION OFFERED BY INDIA

The Government of India shall grant duty free access to all exports from Sri Lanka in respect of items freely importable into India, except on items listed in Annex D of this Agreement, in accordance with the phase out schedule detailed below:

1. Upon entry into force of the Agreement :

    a. Zero duty access for the items in Annexure 'E'
    b. 50% margin of preference on the remaining items except on items listed in Annexure D. Concessions on items in Chapters 51 to 56, 58 to 60 and 63 shall be restricted to 25%.

2. The margin of preference on the items mentioned in (b) above shall be increased to 100% in two stages within three years of the coming into force of the Agreement, except for the textiles items referred to in 1(b) above.

ANNEXURE 'B'

Concession offered by Sri Lanka Government of Sri Lanka shall provide tariff concessions on exports from India to Sri Lanka in respect of items freely importable into Sri Lanka, as detailed below:

1. Zero duty for the items in Annex 'F'-I, upon entering into force of the Agreement.
2. 50% margin of preference for the items in Annex 'F'–II, upon coming into force of the Agreement. The margin of preference in respect of these items shall be deepened to 70%, 90% and 100%, respectively, at the end of the first, second and third year of the entry into force of the Agreement.

3. For the remaining items except those in Annex 'D', the tariffs shall be brought down by not less than 35% before the expiry of three years and 70% before the expiry of the sixth year and 100% before the expiry of eight years, from the date of entry into force of the Agreement.

CONCESSION OFFERED BY SRI LANKA

ANNEXURE 'C'

RULES OF ORIGIN

1. *Short title/commencement*
   These rules may be called the rules of Determination of Origin of Goods under the Free Trade Agreement between the Democratic Socialistic Republic of Sri Lanka and the Republic of India.

2. *Application*
   These rules shall apply to products consigned from the territory of either of the Contracting Parties.

3. *Determination of Origin*
   No product shall be deemed to be the produce or manufacture of either country unless the conditions specified in these rules are complied with in relation to such products, to the satisfaction of the appropriate Authority.

4. *Claim at the time of importation*
   The importer of the product shall, at the time of importation:
   a. make a claim that the products are the produce or manufacture of the country from which they are imported and such products are eligible for preferential treatment under the Agreement, and
   b. produce the evidence specified in these rules.

5. *Originating products*
   Products covered by the Agreement imported into the territory of a Contracting Party from another Contracting Party which are consigned directly within the meaning of rule 9 hereof, shall be eligible for preferential treatment if they conform to the origin requirement under any one of the following conditions:

a. Products wholly produced or obtained in the territory of the exporting Contracting Party as defined in rule 6; or
b. Products not wholly produced or obtained in the territory of the exporting Contracting Party, provided that the said products are eligible under rule 7 or rule 8.

6. *Wholly produced or obtained*

Within the meaning of rule 5(a), the following shall be considered as wholly produced or obtained in the territory of the exporting Contracting Party:

a. raw or mineral products extracted from its soil, its water or its seabed;
b. vegetable products harvested there;
c. animals born and raised there;
d. products obtained from animals referred to in clause (c) above;
e. products obtained by hunting or fishing conducted there;
f. products of sea fishing and other marine products from the high seas by its vessels 3,4;
g. products processed and/or made on board its factory ships exclusively from products referred to in clause (f) above 4, 5;
h. used articles collected there, fit only for the recovery of raw materials;
i. waste and scrap resulting from manufacturing operations conducted there;
j. products extracted from the seabed or below seabed which is situated outside its territorial waters, provided that it has exclusive exploitation rights;
k. goods produced there exclusively from the products referred to in clauses (a) to (j) above.

7. *Not wholly produced or obtained*

a. Within the meaning of rule 5(b), products worked on or processed as a result of which the total value of the materials, parts or produce originating from countries other than the Contracting Parties or of undetermined origin used does not exceed 65% of the f.o.b. value of the products produced or obtained and the final process of manufacture is performed within the territory of the exporting Contracting Party shall be eligible for preferential treatment, subject to the provisions of clauses (b), (c), (d) and (e) of rule 7 and rule 8.

b. Non-originating materials shall be considered to be sufficiently worked or processed when the product obtained is classified in a heading, at the four digit level, of the Harmonised Commodity Description and Coding System different from those in which all the non-originating materials used in its manufacture are classified.

c. In order to determine whether a product originates in the territory of a Contracting Party, it shall not be necessary to establish whether the power and fuel, plant and equipment, and machines and tools used to obtain such products originate in third countries or not.

d. The following shall in any event be considered as insufficient working or processing to confer the status of originating products, whether or not there is a change of heading:

1. Operations to ensure the preservation of products in good condition during transport and storage (ventilation, spreading out, drying, chilling, placing in salt, sulphur dioxide or other aqueous solutions, removal of damaged parts, and like operations);
2. Simple operations consisting of removal of dust, sifting or screening, sorting, classifying, matching (including the making-up of sets of articles), washing, painting, cutting up;
3. (i) changes of packing and breaking up and assembly of consignments,
   (ii) simple slicing, cutting and repacking or placing in bottles, flasks, bags, boxes, fixing on cards or boards, etc., and all other simple packing operations;
4. the affixing of marks, labels or other like distinguishing signs on products or their packaging;
5. simple mixing of products, whether or not of different kinds, where one or more components of the mixture do not meet the conditions laid down in these Rules to enable them to be considered as originating products;
6. simple assembly of parts of products to constitute a complete product;

7. a combination of two or more operations specified in (a) to (f);
8. slaughter of animals;

e. The value of the non-originating materials, parts or produce shall be:

   i. The c.i.f. value at the time of importation of the materials, parts or produce where this can be proven; or
   ii. The earliest ascertainable price paid for the materials, parts or produce of undetermined origin in the territory of the Contracting Parties where the working or processing takes place.

8. *Cumulative rules of origin*
In respect of a product, which complies with the origin requirements provided in rule 5(b) and is exported by any Contracting Party and which has used material, parts or products originating in the territory of the other Contracting Party, the value addition in the territory of the exporting Contracting Party shall be not less than 25 per cent of the f.o.b. value of the product under export subject to the condition that the aggregate value addition in the territories of the Contracting Parties is not less than 35 per cent of the f.o.b. value of the product under export.

9. *Direct consignment*
The following shall be considered to be directly consigned from the exporting country to the importing country:
   a. if the products are transported without passing through the territory of any country other than the countries of the Contracting Parties.
   b. The products whose transport involves transit through one or more intermediate countries with or without transhipment or temporary storage in such countries; provided that
      i. the transit entry is justified for geographical reason or by considerations related exclusively to transport requirements;
      ii. the products have not entered into trade or consumption there; and
      iii. the products have not undergone any operation there other than unloading and reloading or any operation required to keep them in good condition.

10. *Treatment of packing*

    When determining the origin of products, packing should be considered as forming a whole with the product it contains. However, packing may be treated separately if the national legislation so requires.

11. *Certificate of origin*

    Products eligible for a Certificate of origin in the form annexed shall support preferential treatment issued by an authority designated by the Government of the exporting country and notified to the other country in accordance with the certification procedures to be devised and approved by both the Contracting Parties.

12. *Prohibitions*

    Either country may prohibit importation of products containing any inputs originating from States with which it does not have economic and commercial relations;

13. *Co-operation between contracting parties*

    a. The Contracting Parties will do their best to co-operate in order to specify origin of inputs in the Certificate of Origin.
    b. The Contracting Parties will take measures necessary to address, to investigate and, where appropriate, to take legal and/or administrative action to prevent circumvention of this Agreement through false declaration concerning country of origin or falsification of original documents.
    c. Both the Contracting Parties will co-operate fully, consistent with their domestic laws and procedures, in instances of circumvention or alleged circumvention of the Agreement to address problems arising from circumvention including facilitation of joint plant visits and contacts by representatives of both Contracting Parties upon request and on a case-by-case basis.
    d. If either Party believes that the rules of origin are being circumvented, it may request consultation to address the matter or matters concerned with a view to seeking a mutually satisfactory solution. Each party will hold such consultations promptly.

14. *Review*

    These rules may be reviewed as and when necessary upon request of either Contracting Party and may be open to such modifications as may be agreed upon.

CERTIFICATE OF ORIGIN

<table>
<tr><td colspan="3">1. Goods consigned from
(Exporters' Business Name, Address, Country)</td><td colspan="3">Reference No.
NDO-SRI LANKA FREE TRADE AGREEMENT (ISFTA) (Combined declaration and certificate)
Issued in (Country)
(See notes)</td></tr>
<tr><td colspan="3">2. Goods consigned to
(Consignee's Name, Address, Country)</td><td colspan="3" rowspan="2">4. For Official use</td></tr>
<tr><td colspan="3">3. Means of transport and route
(as far as known)</td></tr>
<tr><td>5. Tariff item number</td><td>6. Marks and numbers of packages</td><td>7. Number and kind of packages: description of goods</td><td>8. Origin criterion (see Notes)</td><td>9. Gross weight of other quantity</td><td>10. Number and date of invoice</td></tr>
<tr><td colspan="3">11. Declaration by the Exporter

The undersigned hereby declares that the above details and statements are correct; That all the goods were produced in (Country) and that they comply with the origin requirements specified for those goods in ISFTA for goods exported to (Importing Country)
Place and date, signature of the authorised signatory</td><td colspan="3">12. Certificate:

It is hereby certified, on the basis of control carried out that the declaration by the exporter is correct.

Place and date, signature and stamp of certifying authority.</td></tr>
</table>

I. To qualify for prefernce, product must:

- fall within a description of products eligible for concessions in the country of destination under this agreement.
- comply with ISFTA Rules of Origin. Each Article in a consignment must qualify separately in its own right; and

- comply with the consignment conditions specified by the ISFTA Rules of Origin. In general products must be consigned directly within the meaning of Rule 9 hereof from the country of exportation to the country of destination.

II. Entries to be made in Box 8

Preference products must be wholly produced or obtained in the exporting Contracting Party in accordance with Rule 6 of the ISFTA Rule of Origin, or where not wholly produced or obtained in the exporting Contracting Party must be eligible under Rule 7 or Rule 8 Products wholly produced or obtained enter the letter 'A' in Box 8.

Products not wholly produced or obtained; the entry in Box 8 should be as follows:

8. Enter letter 'B' in box 8 for products, which meet the origin criterion according to Rule
7. Entry of letter would be followed by the sum of the value of materials, parts or produce originating from non-contracting parties or undetermined origin used, expressed as a percentage of the f.o.b. value of the product (example B ( ) per cent).
9. Enter letter 'C' in Box 8 for products, which meet the origin criteria according to Rule 8. Entry of letter 'C' would be followed by the sum of the aggregate content originating in the territory of the exporting Contracting Party expressed as a percentage of the f.o.b. value of the exported product (example 'C' ( ) per cent).

NOTES

1. Includes mineral fuels, lubricants and related materials as well as mineral or metal ores.
2. Includes agricultural and forestry products.
3. 'Vessels' shall refer to fishing vessels engaged in commercial fishing, registered in the country of the Contracting Party and operated by a citizen or citizens of the Contracting Party or partnership, corporation or association, duly registered in such country, at least 60 per cent of equity of which is owned by a citizen or citizens and/or Government of such Contracting Party or 75 per cent by citizens and/or Governments of the Contracting Parties. However, the products taken from vessels, engaged in commercial fishing under

Bilateral Agreements which provide for chartering/leasing of such vessels and/or sharing of catch between Contracting Party will also be eligible for preferential treatment.

4. In respect of vessels or factory ships operated by Government agencies, the requirements of flying the flag of the Contracting Party does not apply.
5. For the purpose of this Agreement, the term 'factory ship' means any vessel, as defined, used for processing and/or making on board products exclusively from those products referred to in clause (f) of Rule 6.
6. Cumulation as implied by Rule 8 means that only products which have acquired originating status in the territory of one Contracting Party may be taken into account when used as inputs for a finished product eligible for preferential treatment in the territory of the other Contracting Party.

Bibliography

Balachandran, P. K., 'Lankans Filled with Misgivings about Fernandes' Dream': http://k.t.rajasingam.tripod.com/canal.htm

Bhasin, Avtar Singh, ed., *India–Sri Lanka Relations and Sri Lanka's Ethnic Conflict: Documents: 1947–2000*, 5 vols., New Delhi: India Research Press, 2001.

Braun, Dieter, *The Indian Ocean*, New Delhi: Oxford University Press, 1983.

Chaturvedi, Sanjay, 'Resurrecting Maritime South Asia: Critical Perspectives on the 21st Century', in *Reconstructing South Asia: Vision and Mission Ahead*, ed. A. Subramanyam Raju (forthcoming).

Cherian, John, 'A Friend in Need', *Frontline*, vol. 20, no. 12, 7–20 June 2003: http://www.flonnet.com/fl2012/stories/20030620005001700.htm

Doctor, Adi H., 'India's Indian Ocean Policy', *Indian Journal of Political Science* (Chennai), vol. 51, no. 3, July–September 1990, pp. 36–79.

Gunaratne, Rohan, 'Trends in Maritime Terrorism: The Sri Lankan Case': http://www.is.lk/is/spot/sp0316/clip8.html

Jayasinghe, W. T., *Kachchativu and the Maritime Boundary of Sri Lanka*, Colombo: Stamford Lake, 2003.

Kelegama, Saman, 'Sri Lanka Exports to India: Impact of Free Trade Agreement', *Economic and Political Weekly*, vol. 37, no. 30, 26 July 2003, pp. 3153–4.

National Fishworkers Forum, *Charter of Demands 2002*, Thiruvananthapuram: National Fishworkers Forum (NFF), 2002.

Mahendran, Arjuna and Rajive Casie Chitty, 'Hanuman's Bridge: Facilitating Trade and Investment between Sri Lanka and Southern India', *South Asian Survey*, vol. 7, no. 1, 2000, pp. 25–35.

Maritime Zones of India (Regulations of Fishing by Foreign Vessels), Act, 1981 (Act No. 42 of 1981).

Mujtaba, Syed Ali, 'India: Fishing for Trouble', *Himal*, vol. 16, no. 10, October 2003, pp. 9–11.

Muni, S. D., 'Kachchativu Settlement: Befriending Neighbouring Regimes', *Economic and Political Weekly*, vol. 9, no. 28, 13 July 1974, pp. 1119, 1121.

Murthy, Padmaja, 'Indo-Sri Lankan Security Perceptions: Divergence and Convergences': http://www.idsa-india org/an-may-08.html

Morell, B. James, *The Law of the Sea*, Jefferson, Missouri: McFarland, 1992.

Naik, Anant V., Sajal Ghosh and V. Raghuraman, *Energy Security Issues and India*, July 2003: http://www.acus.org/energy

Subramanian, Nirupama, 'To Nowhere Land', *Frontline*, vol. 19, no. 15, 20 July–2 August 2002: http://www.frontlineonnet.com/fl1915/19150680.htm

Panikkar, K. M., *India and the Indian Ocean*, Bombay [now Mumbai]: George Allen Unwin, 1945.

Rajasingham, K. T., 'A Canal…and an Island…!', 28 August 2002, *Asian Tribune*: http://www.asiantribune.com/show_article.php?id=25

Raju, A. Subramanyam, 'French Economic and Strategic Interests in the Western Indian Ocean Region: 1975–1990', *Journal of Indian Ocean Studies*, vol. 5, no. 1, November 1997, pp. 21–34.

———, 'The Politics of US Militarization of the Indian Ocean: India's Response', in *Democracies at Loggerheads: Security Aspects of US–India Relations*, ed. Raju, A. Subramanyam Raju, Colorado: International Academic Publishers, and New Delhi: South Asian Publishers, 2001, pp. 75–100.

———, 'Women and Terrorism in South Asia: Some Observations', in *Terrorism in South Asia: Views from India*, ed. A. Subramanyam Raju, Singapore: Marshal Cavendish, pp. 227–37, and New Delhi: India Research Press, 2004, pp. 328–30.

———, 'Energy Cooperation in South Asia', in *Energy Security and the Indian Ocean*, ed. Dennis Rumely and Sanjay Chaturvedi, New Delhi: South Asian Publishers, 2005, pp. 190–203.

———, 'Maritime Cooperation in South Asia', in *Reconstructing South Asia: Problems and Perspectives*, ed. A. Subramanyam Raju (forthcoming).

———, 'Indian Fishermen (In)Security in Indo-Sri Lankan Waters' in *Human Security in India: Conflict in the New Age of Insecurity*, ed. Santishree Pandit (forthcoming).

———, 'India's Security in the Palk Bay Straits', in *Security Dimensions of Peninsular India*, ed. Gopalji Malviya, Chennai: Centre for Security Analysis, 2005 (forthcoming).

———, 'Sethusamudram Ship Canal Project: Problems and Prospects', *Indian Ocean Survey*, vol. 1, no. 2, July–December 2005, pp. 105–8.

Rao, S. L., *Indian Ocean: Challenges and Opportunities*, New Delhi: Navy Foundation, 1992.

Sambandan, V. S., 'The LTTE's Blueprint', *Frontline*, 21 November 2003, vol. 20, no. 23, pp. 12–14.

Sarvananthan, Muttukrishna, 'Contraband Trade and Unofficial Capital Transfers between Sri Lanka and India', *Economic and Political Weekly*, 23 July 1994, vol. 29, no. 30, pp. 1948–56.

Simmondes, Kenneth R., *New Directions in the Law of the Sea*, London: Oceana Publications, 1988.

Singh, K.R., 'Sri Lanka—Evolution of Naval Strategy', *Journal of Indian Ocean Studies*, vol. 10, no. 1, April 2002, pp. 91–9.

Suryanarayan, V. *Kachchativu and the Problems of Indian Fishermen in the Palk Bay Region*, Chennai: T. R. Publications, 1994.

'Stepping Stone to a Separate State', *Frontline*, 21 November 2003, p. 15.

Vijayalakshmi, Chandrahasan Anne Nirmala, 'The Application to Sri Lanka of the Emerging New Regime of the Law of the Sea, in Relation to the Delimitation of Sri Lanka's Maritime Boundaries and Jurisdiction over Sea Zone, and Areas of the Seabed', unpublished Ph.D. thesis, Colombo: University of Colombo, 1983.

Vivekanandan, V., 'Crossing Maritime Borders: The Problem and Solution in the Indo-Sri Lankan Context', in *Forging Unity: Coastal Communities and the Indian Ocean's Future*, ed. K.G. Kumar, Chennai: International Collective in Support of Fishworkers, 2003, pp. 76–89.

RCSS PUBLICATIONS

- *Defence, Technology and Cooperative Security in South Asia: Report on the Proceedings of the Tenth Summer Workshop* (RCSS, 2004)
- *Environment Development and Human Security: Perspectives from South Asia* (2003)
- *Terrorism in South Asia: Impact on Development and Democratic Process* (SIPRA, 2003)
- *South Asia and the War on Terrorism* (India Research Press, 2003)
- *Shaping the Future—A South Asian Civil Society Dialogue* (RCSS, July 2002)
- *Small Arms and Human Insecurity* (RCSS, July 2002)
- *SAARC in the Twenty-First Century: Towards a Cooperative Future* (July 2002)
- *Memories of a Genocidal Partition: The Haunting Tale of Victims, Witnesses and Perpetrators* (RCSS, July 2002)
- *South Asian Security Futures: A Dialogue of Director's Regional Strategic Studies Institutes* (March 2002)
- *Security and Governance in South Asia* (September 2001)
- *Globalization and Non-Traditional Security in South Asia* (September 2001)
- *Security in the New Millennium* (India Research Press, 2001)
- *The Simla Agreement 1972: Its Wasted Promise* (Manohar, 2001)

RCSS Newsletter

A quarterly bulletin, it publishes a brief report of RCSS activities, presentations at its workshops on topics of contemporary interest and news and programmes of the RCSS and its alumnae.

RCSS Policy Studies

36. Maritime Cooperation between India and Sri Lanka (Manohar, 2006)
35 Nuclear Risk Reduction Measures in South Asia: Problems and Prospects (Manohar, 2006)
34 Indo-Pak Conflicts: Ripe to Resolve? (Manohar, 2005)
33 Small Arms and the Security Debate in South Asia (Manohar, 2005)
32 New Nuclear Triangle and China's Role in South Asia (RCSS: 2005)
31 Stability through Economic Cooperation in a Nuclear Environment (Manohar, 2005)
30 Multi-Track Diplomacy between India and Pakistan: A Conceptual Framework for Sustainable Security (Manohar, 2005)
29 The Role of Mediation in Resolving India-Pakistan Conflict: Parameters and Possibilities (Manohar, 2005)
28 HIV/AIDS as a Security Threat to India (Manohar, 2005)
27 Nepal's Maoist Movement and Implications for India and China (Manohar, 2005)
26 Elite Perceptions in Foreign Policy: Role of Print Media in Influencing India-Pakistan Relations, 1989–1999 (Manohar, 2004)
25 Nuclar Risk Reduction Measures and Restraint Regime in South Asia (Manohar, 2004)
24 River Water Sharing Problem Between India and Pakistan: Case Study of the Indus Basin Water Treaty (June 2004)

Fellowship in South Asian Alternatives (FISAA) Monograph

- Water, Power And People: A South Asian Manifesto on the Politics and Knowledge of Water (1997)
- The Nuclear Debate: Ironies and Immoralities (1998)

Others

- *Directory of Individuals and Institutions Engaged in South Asian Strategic Studies* (1998).